GENEALOGICAL RESEARCH IN ENGLAND AND WALES

VOLUME 3

OLD ENGLISH HANDWRITING, LATIN, RESEARCH STANDARDS AND PROCEDURES

by

David E. Gardner
Frank Smith

BOOKCRAFT
Salt Lake City, Utah

Copyright

Bookcraft, Inc.

1964

LITHOGRAPHED IN U.S.A.

BY

PUBLISHERS PRESS

SALT LAKE CITY   UTAH

CONTENTS

Section One

Section Two

CHAPTER

Volume IV will include a description of sources such
as Apprentice Records — Freeman (City and Burgess)
Records — Manor Court Rolls — Chancery Proceed-
ings — Registers of Schools and Universities — Quarter
Sessions Records — Directories of Cities, Towns and
Counties — Poll Books and Elections — Feet of Fines
— etc.

Foreword

The authors' original plan was to have two chapters on handwriting as part of a larger Volume 3, which would also have included a description of sources such as apprentice records, records of freemen, manor court rolls, inquisitions post mortem, and many other valuable records.

The microfilming of millions of pages of original records means that more and more people are coming face to face with the problems of deciphering old documents. This prompted the decision to explain in more detail the problem of reading old English scripts.

It was also felt necessary to include an elementary chapter on Latin as related to parish registers, since much original material is written in Latin.

Now that many people have studied Volumes 1 and 2 and have become familiar with those sources and how to use them, it was felt necessary to include, at this point, a chapter on research standards and procedures. Students have now reached the point where they need help in determining when a possible connection can be accepted or when it cannot.

In order that this reference material can be carried as a smaller book, descriptions of additional genealogical sources have been deferred to a fourth volume.

Appreciation is here expressed to all who advised or assisted in the preparation of this volume.

Special mention is made of Mr. R. Sharpe France, County Archivist for Lancashire, for choosing and deciphering representative documents for the chapters on handwriting; to the National Library of Wales for similar services; and to Miss C. L. M. Horner for help in preparing the chapter on Latin.

SECTION
ONE

CHAPTER ONE

Introduction to Old English Handwriting

Some people receive a shock and a disappointment when they discover that the style of handwriting of our more remote ancestors is quite different from ours. Nevertheless, research in the records of the past is essential if true pedigrees are to be constructed. Consequently every record searcher has to learn to read the various types of handwriting, become acquainted with terminology and abbreviations, recognize simple Latin and understand the problems arising out of dialectal and phonetic spellings.

For centuries Latin was the language used in the preparation of official records, and except for the period 1651-1660, during the Commonwealth, Latin was used in all formal documents. It was not until 1733 that the law forbade the use of Latin and ordered that all official documents be written in English. For a short time, however, some parish registers continued to be written in Latin, but generally Latin was abandoned many years before 1733 in parish registers.

The microfilming of millions of pages of original records means that more and more record searchers are able, because of photography, to view vast quantities of original documents. Primarily we are interested in handwriting found in documents written after 1500, for it was in 1538 that parish registers were first introduced[1] and it is after that time that the majority of probate courts[1] have existing records. The same handwriting was used for Latin as for English, but apart from the Latin which may be fairly easily recognized and translated in parish registers, marriage bonds, and some probate records,[2] the searcher may have to leave Latin documents alone until he has studied that language.

The late Arthur M. Burke called for prudence in the deciphering of old handwriting when he wrote: "A special knowledge is necessary to decipher accurately the early entries, and the extracts of unqualified searchers are seldom to be relied upon. Indeed some of the printed registers [of parishes] are not above suspicion in this respect, and reference to the original is often most advisable."[3]

Handwriting

Although there were established forms of handwriting in ancient times, personal characteristics in the handwriting of private correspondents differed then just as they do now. The exception to this was

---

[1]*See* Smith & Gardner: *Genealogical Research in England and Wales* (Salt Lake City: 1962), Vol. I, chaps. 10-13, for parish registers, and Vol. 2, chap. 3, p. 60, for probates.
[2]*Ibid.* Vol. 2. See illustrations on pages 59-60, 64-65, 78-81, 94-102, 125-126.
[3]Arthur M. Burke: *Key To The Ancient Parish Registers of England and Wales,* (London: 1908), page 24.

the handwriting of the professional scribes who had been given a strict training in the art of handwriting and adhered to the use of the strict forms of script. To the remaining few who could write, handwriting was often a tedious and laborious task just as it is to many people today.

Compulsory education in England and Wales was introduced less than a century ago.[4] Those who learned to write before that time were generally taught in day schools established by local voluntary effort, in charity schools, or in Sunday Schools. Many were self-taught. The wealthy sent their children either to day or boarding schools, sometimes known as "grammar schools" and "academies," or employed a private governess or tutor. There are no statistics listing the percentage of persons unable to write but the *Marriage* Act of 1753 provided that the bridegroom, bride, and witnesses sign their names or make their marks in the marriage register at the conclusion of the ceremony.[5] From this date it is possible to surmise how many adults were able to write. A study made of the marriage registers of four parishes in northern Lincolnshire showed that in 1760 only about forty percent of the couples could write at the time of marriage. By 1800 this had increased to forty-eight percent, by 1850 to sixty percent, and by 1890 it was said to have increased to over ninety percent.[6]

Broadly speaking, the types of handwriting found in parish records and probate court records between 1540 and 1900 are the *Court Hands*, the *Secretary Hands*, and the *Italic Hands*, and in the more modern records the so-called *English Round Hands*. There will be found varying versions and mixtures of these types, the reading of which depends on the style of the individual writer, local customs and the period.

With some study and a little practice, most people will be able to read reasonably legible handwriting written after 1700. With more experience most documents written in Court, Secretary, and Italic hands in the English language can be read back to the sixteenth century. The reading of handwriting also consists of the ability to recognize what was intended by the writer. Common sense and a few hours of practice are essential in order to read most of the words, but there is some danger of mechanically copying instead of using common sense as a guide, and it would be well to have this text-book close by for reference. Sometimes the reader will jump to a conclusion as to the spelling of a name because it looks familiar, whereas closer and more careful inspection may disclose it to be something entirely different.

One of the soundest ways to ensure success in understanding documents is to learn something of the method of recording (the business

---

[4] Education Act of Great Britain, 1870.
[5] *See* Volume 1, p. 160, with examples of signed marriage entries on pages 181 and 210.
[6] R. C. Russell, *A History of Schools and Education in Barton-on-Humber,* 1800-1850, (Barton: 1960).

methods) of the period, person or court concerned; to study the topography, geography, place-names,[7] history and tradition,[8] as well as
the names of principal families,[9] of the area and period in which the
research is being conducted. Students are urged to consult books
dealing with the records they wish to read. There is a *free* catalog
for all official British Government record publications.[10] The student
should also read prefaces and introductions to these official publications
and those found in other printed calendars, indexes and histories pub-
lished by county history, archaeology and record societies and by the
British Record Society.[11] It is well worthwhile to find out whether a
portion of a parish register or other record has been printed and to read
the prefaces before attempting to read the original records or their
photo-copies.

It is necessary to transcribe accurately the relevant information,
and that means that nothing is to be added or left out. If there is
any doubt as to the sense and meaning of the information abstracted
it is far better to transcribe the whole of the document and make a
thorough study of it later. Any peculiarities appearing in documents
searched should be commented upon in your notes so that the transcription may be clearly understood.

It is wise to read documents with caution as there was no accepted form of spelling of names of persons and places until comparatively recent times. It is therefore impossible to state how much allow-
ance for spelling eccentricities must be made because the recordings
might be the result of dictation affected by accent and local dialect.
There will always be a margin of error to be considered.

In Wales and Monmouthshire, where the Welsh language is spoken,
the majority of the official records are in English and Latin, but the
Welsh given names and place-names are frequently written in Welsh.
There is, however, an abundance of records, mainly of the Nonconformist denominations, written in Welsh.

---

[7]*The Publications of the English Place-Name Society,* (Cambridge: The University
   Press, 1924-   ) and other publication dealing with place-names.

[8]*The Victoria History of the Counties of England* is a national historic survey designed
   to cover the history of every county and many of the principal families.

[9]*Ibid.* Also *The Dictionary of National Biography,* (London: 1906 and other editions).
   Also, G.E.C., *The Complete Peerage,* (London: St. Catherine Press, 1910-1953), and
   other works on Landed Gentry, Baronetage, Peerage, etc.

[10]*Record Publications,* Government Publications Sectional List No. 24 of 57 pages, ob-
   tainable *gratis* from H. M. Stationery Office, York House, Kingsway, London, W.C. 2,
   England. It includes publications relating to the British Isles, the American colonies
   and elsewhere.

[11]*Op. cit.* Vol. 2, chap. 9, pp. 195-307 lists all English and Welsh counties together with
   listings of publications relating to records in each county, including guides to county
   record offices.

Writing Surfaces and Materials

Paper has been in use as a writing surface from before the four-teenth century but parchment has been preferred for official business for hundreds of years. Generally, paper did not come into frequent use until the sixteenth century, but official concern in the preservation of records is reflected in the Act of Parliament of 1597 ordering every parish minister to copy existing registers into a new book of parchment. Until that time many registers were of paper. In most parishes where the minister failed to copy the paper records, the paper has perished and the register is lost. This does not mean that parchment was the only material used in the making of records because there are in Public Record Office, London, and elsewhere, many records written on paper contemporaneously with parchment.

Parchment used in ancient records was made from the skins of sheep and goats, and vellum — a word coined to describe parchment made from veal — was not only made from calves, but also from lambs and kids. The skins were soaked, rubbed and scraped to remove hair, and then stretched to make them thinner. The finished product is darker and somewhat brown on the hair side and whiter and smoother on the flesh side. These distinctions are visible and account for some vari-ances in contrast in reading original and photo-copied documents.

Until the nineteenth century the majority of pens consisted of swan, goose, turkey and crow quills cut or sharpened to the angle necessary to hold the quill and apply it to the writing surface. Metal nibs or pen points, allowing greater flexibility in handwriting, did not come into general use until after 1830.

Most inks prior to 1500 were made from the galls of oak trees and iron salts and gum, but at a later date carbon was introduced into the mixtures and inks were of varying qualities. As the carbon ink merely rested on the surface and did not stain the parchment or paper it was liable to flake off but the outline of the letters scratched by the quill might still be visible. Faded records exist, however, because of the use of inferior materials such as inks that were weakened by thinning. Documents folded for many years have become worn at the folds caus-ing illegibilities, and some records have been damaged by poor handling, by rats or mice, by insects, and by damp and fire. Many are dirty because of age and neglect.

Sometimes unfamiliar handwriting, faded ink or damaged docu-ments, make it impossible to decipher more than 50% of the letters of a word and the brain must supply the rest of the word from its stored knowledge. Here, however, one must be cautious about making wrong interpretations, but there is much that can be done if the right back-ground is accumulated and a careful evaluation of the record is made.

Patience and perseverance are always a necessary asset in reading old records.

Terminology

In describing a manuscript various terms are used, among which are the following:[12]

Document — may consist of a single sheet, or a number of pieces or sheets fastened together. A book into which a number of records have been copied as a unit may also be called a document.

File — may be a single document of several sheets or a number of documents filed together.

Roll — a document or documents preserved on a roll or by rolling. Some documents called rolls are technically files or books.

Book or Volume or Register — a number of leaves or folios laid one on the other and sewn together. Some are found described as *libro* or *liber*.

Folio — a leaf of a book or manuscript, one or a number of pages; a quire of four doubled sheets giving eight leaves and sixteen pages.[13]

Leaf — usually a page out of a book. Pieces of parchment or paper are often described as "pieces or sheets" of parchment or paper, and if they are part of a book they should be called leaves or folios.

Membrane — a piece of parchment. If several are laid flat and attached they may form a file, or bound together they may form a book, volume or register.

Face — the inner surface of the membrane known as the "face of the roll"; the flesh side or the right side or the white side of the membrane.

Dorse — the back of a document, page, or membrane; the outer surface, the hair side, or the wrong or black side of the membrane.[13]

Recto — the right hand page or front of a leaf.

Verso — the left hand page or back of a leaf.

Foliation — the number of leaves or folios in a book or manuscript.

Pagination — the marking, numbering, or making into pages.

---

[12]Additional information is to be found in the "Report on Editing Historical Documents" in *Bulletin of the Institute of Historical Research,* (London: 1925) Vol. 1, pp. 6-25. There is also a useful list of terminology in this present series, Vol. 2, pp. 30-33.

[13]See also Vol. 2, pp. 29-30.

Suggestions to Instructor

1. Lay stress on the importance of investigation into the subject and the need of practice and perseverance.

2. Stimulate the class members to read all that is available pertinent to the subject.

3. Anything worth having is worth working for. Motivate the group to accept serious mental effort as the proper price for proficiency in this genealogical endeavor.

"Genius is two percent inspiration and ninety percent perspiration."

—Thomas A. Edison

CHAPTER TWO

Spellings and Abbreviations

Capital letters and place-names are usually difficult to decipher, but as capital letters do not stand alone they might be deciphered by making sense of the rest of the word, though care must be taken not to make a wrong interpretation of the first letter since this will produce an entirely different name. Non-existent, or unsystematic punctuation was a general feature; and writers were very lax in the use of the *period* (.), the *virgula* (/), and the *comma* (,). Sometimes ordinary words beginning with a capital letter are found in the middle of a sentence.

It should be clearly understood that until comparatively recent times there was no universally accepted way of spelling a word, the name of a person, or a place-name, which were written as they sounded to the recorder, i.e., written phonetically. Phonetic recordings were influenced by the dialect or accent used by the informant, and in some manuscripts scribes have spelled words in several different ways on the same page. The hearing ability and the native background of the recorder, who may have understood or heard only a part of what was said, played an important part in what was finally written down.

The effect of a dialect upon the written word is illustrated in a record of two centuries ago wherein a native of Glodwick near Oldham, Lancashire, was recorded as born in *Glatit*, near *Owdum*, because that is the dialectal or phonetic spelling of what the recorder heard. In another old document the place of birth of an ancestor was given as *Learden*. This eventually proved to be Henley-in-Arden, Warwickshire, the clerk apparently having heard only snatches of the place-name. Similarly Bromwich becomes *Brommidge* and Adwick becomes *Addick*.

In Welsh research the situation is aggravated by language differences. Welshmen born in Bodfari, Rhosllanerchrugog, or Machynlleth, have been found recorded from their verbal statements as being born in *Potphari*, *Rosannaswgregog*, and *Mahendraeth* respectively.

Abbreviations

In order to save time and space many scribes used abbreviations. These may prove to be temporary impediments for the beginner because the scribe may have written only one or two letters of each syllable of the word and the rest of the letters have to be supplied by the reader. This is especially true in Latin documents. The abbreviations used in English manuscripts are generally easy to learn and it is hoped that the following explanation will eliminate these impediments as regards these manuscripts.

1. *Contractions* leave out one or more letters in the *middle* of the word and this action is indicated by various strokes, signs or other marks, and sometimes by the apostrophe ('). A mark may consist of a dash or wavy line placed over short letters or passing through the upstrokes (ascenders) of tall letters or the downstrokes (descenders) of others. Such a line placed above vowels or the consonants *m* or *n* may indicate the omission of certain vowels or possibly an additional *m* or *n*, so that "remẽbrance," "com͂ittee," "Clem͂et," and "Johañes," stand for *remembrance, committee, Clement,* and *Johannes* respectively.

The contractions associated with the letter *p* are quite common, so that a mark, usually a dash or wavy line, above or through the down-stroke of the *p* (p or p̃) indicate *per, par, pre,* and sometimes *pro.* For example, "P̃ish" or "pish," "p̃fect" or "pfect," and "p̃sents" or "psents," are abbreviations for *parish, perfect,* or *presents.* Similar marks are found in "Edͧus" for *Edmondus,* and "Edͦrus" for *Edwardus,* and "Johͪnes" for *Johannes.*

The apostrophe (') came into use as a convenient substitute for abbreviation marks, so that "p'fect," "P'ish," "Edm'nd's," and "M'gareta," stand for *perfect, parish, Edmundus* and *Margareta.* Even surnames were contracted; example of these are "Penithor'e" for *Penithorne* and "Lamb't" for *Lambert.*

2. *Superior Letters.* The use of these is another form of contraction or suspension. This consisted of omitting a letter or letters from a word and raising some of the letters above the line. Thus *wᵗʰ* and *wᶜʰ* represent *with* and *which.* Yᵗ and yᵉ represent *that* and *the,* the "y" being a survival of the Thorn, a letter found in ancient alphabets, which had the pronunciation of *th* and was written somewhat like a letter *y.*

Many given names are shown in abbreviated form. Examples of these are "Jnᵒ," usually for *John,* and "Richʳd" for *Richard.* Surnames are often abbreviated. For example "Chamʳˢ" will often appear for *Chambers.* The present day titles of *Mʳ* and *Mʳˢ* are a survival of this practice, although "Mʳ" and "mʳ" may mean *master* in old records. In official documents the monarch may be referred to as *His Maᵗⁱᵉ* for *His Majesty.*

3. *Suspensions* leave off the final letters of a word and this action is usually indicated by the use of a period (.), a colon (:), various strokes, signs, or marks, or sometimes the apostrophe ('). The oldest form of suspension was the use of the initial letter of a word, thus *R* was the abbreviation for *Recipe,* a sign still displayed by druggists at prescription centers.

The use of a dot or period (.) in suspension is illustrated by "wid.", "Phil.", and "ite.", which mean *widow, Philip,* and *item.* The use of a colon (:) is noted in "f:" and "fa:", the first meaning either *filia* or *filius* (daughter or son), and the second *filia* (daughter). It is unfortunate, however, that some writers did not trouble to record the period or mark, leaving some ambiguity as to meaning. The given name of Philipa or Phillipa for a girl is common in Cornwall, and a parish register entry giving

Phil f John Bawden

leaves a distinct uncertainty as to whether or not the child was Philipa, a *daughter* or Philip, a *son.*

The dash or wavy lines are also used to indicate suspensions, with "Rad" and "Ric" representing *Radulphus* and *Ricardus*, and "hi" representing *him.* In some documents the apostrophe (') will be used as in *Ric'* for *Richard* and the surname *Rushton* will be abbreviated to *Rushto'.*

In Latin documents the suspensions indicate final letters omitted, but writers of English documents who were also constantly using Latin would, out of habit, place an unnecessary suspension mark at the end of a complete English word that might have been abbreviated had it been written in Latin. It is important therefore to note that suspension marks do *not* necessarily indicate abbreviations.

It was common to add a letter *e* at the end of words without any apparent reason. Examples are *sicke* for *sick, welle* for *well,* and *Marye* for *Mary. Mary* will also be found recorded as *Marie* where the *i* has been used instead of the *y* and an *e* added at the end. This must not be confused with the modern name of *Marie.*

As an example of these abbreviations and signs, pages from the *original* parish registers of Whalley, Lancashire, have been reproduced, together with the same entries as they appear in the *printed* registers[1] of Whalley. (See pages 33-38)

Study these carefully as a means of orientation and training.[2]

Suggestions to Instructor

Drawing from personal experience or text books other than this one:[3]

1. Prepare a list of given names, surnames, and places in phonetic or dialect versions. Have the class attempt to give the correct versions.

---

[1] *The Parish Registers of Whalley, Lancs.,* (Lancashire Parish Register Society, vol. 74: (1936).

[2] *See* op. cit. Vol. I, page 154 for another example of an original page of a parish register (Bury, Lancs.) and its transcription.

[3] Use *Genealogical Research in England and Wales,* vol. 1, pages 48, 55, 61, 179-180 (for variations of spelling); pages 176 & 179 (for bad transcriptions); pages 125, 130-132, 137, 145, 153-154, 181, 198-199, 201, 207, 210, 216-217 (for photo illustrations); pages 272-276 (for dialect). Vol. 2, pages 59 ,61, 65, 68-69, 78-81, 95, 98, 102, 126 (for photo illustrations). Use the "Short List of Books For Detailed Study and Reference" at end of this text-book, some of these will be in libraries.

2. List examples of abbreviated words not used in this chapter and have the class complete the words. Use contractions, superior letters, and suspensions.

3. Listing additional words not given in the chapter, use the special abbreviation signs and have the class complete the words.

CHAPTER THREE

Alphabets

It is essential to learn the various forms of each letter, and particularly the capital letters, of the alphabet, but the mere memorizing of alphabets is only one step in the understanding of handwriting. While practicing on these alphabets a study should be made of original or photo-copied documents whose texts are printed verbatim.[1] However, the student must not expect to read several words at a glance immediately upon learning these various forms of letters, but he will be able to recognize letters in words and by exercising patience will come to read whole words.

In reading difficult texts it is well to beware of making too fanciful a guess. Rather than take a word for granted it is better to transcribe it letter by letter. Difficult letters in words that cannot at first be read should be compared with letters in words that have been identified. If a word is not recognized, leave a gap in the transcript and after the majority of the document has been copied and the writing style has become familiar it may be possible to fill in the gaps when the sense of the text is understood.

On page 13 is an example of alphabets showing *Chancery, Court,* and *Secretary* hands.[2]

On page 14 is "General Alphabet of the Old Law Hands" illustrating a variety of forms of letters, mainly but not entirely from the 16th and 17th centuries' *Legal* and *Chancery* Hands.[3]

On pages 17-26 are the twenty alphabets of the 15th to the 17th centuries.[4]

This display of a variety of alphabets furnishes information on the differences found in old English handwriting and shows that it may be difficult to determine what styles are used if the writer mixed the various forms.

A good way to become familiar with the letter forms in handwriting is to prepare a list of some of the more commonly used forms of letters found in some of the documents used in genealogical research and write the letters several hundred times. An exercise in this is found

---

[1]A number of useful books having photo-copies and transcripts will be found in the bibliography of this book. *See* also chapter 1, footnote 3.

[2]A. F. Bennett, *A Guide for Genealogical Research* (Salt Lake City: 1951), p. 268.

[3]Leaflet based on A. Wright's *Court-Hand Restored* (London: 1818 and other editions) in H. E. P. Grieve's *Examples of English Handwriting 1150-1750* (Chelmsford, Essex: Essex Record Office Publications No. 21, 1954), price $2. (Highly recommended)

[4]Sir Hilary Jenkinson, *The Later Court Hands in England From the Fifteenth to the Seventeenth Century* (Cambridge: University Press, 1927), part 2.

on pages 27-32. Using a soft pencil, copy each letter several times, then erase and write them again. Keep repeating this procedure until the characters are firmly fixed in the mind. Then close the book and attempt to write the complete alphabet from memory. If this is conscientiously done for the letters used in *Secretary* and *Court* hands these letters will become familiar.

In the various alphabets appearing in this chapter it will be noticed that there are some letters which appear similar to a letter in a modern alphabet but that they represent an entirely different letter. It would be wise to make a list of these as you study the alphabets. Some obvious ones are the *Secretary Hand e* which often looks like the modern *o*; the *Court Hand c* which often looks like the modern *r*; and the *Court Hand r* which often looks like the modern *w*.

Numerals

It was usual to use Latin, i.e., Roman numerals in old English records. Arabic figures were first used to number the folios, in showing the year, in indexes and notes, but the old system of using Roman numerals continued even down into the 19th century and followed the normal handwriting styles being used by the writer.

Illustrations of the Roman numerals are shown on pages 31-32. A useful table of references for Roman numerals, cardinals and ordinals will be found on pages 93-94.

The Twenty Examples of Alphabets

For those who wish to learn why there are as many as twenty alphabets in use during the 16th and 17th centuries, the following notes are a brief explanation.

The study of handwriting might commence with the decree of 789 A.D. when the Emperor Charlemagne ordered a revision of certain books, the result of which was the development of a better form of handwriting which is known as the Caroline Miniscule. This is the type of handwriting found in the Domesday Book compiled by order of William the Conqueror about 1086.

The handwriting found in the British Isles for sometime after the Norman Conquest (1066) is generally divided into two main classes, which nevertheless had a common origin. The first is the *Book Hand* or *Text Hand* which was used in literary and church manuscripts compiled for reading by scholars. The second is the *Charter Hand* used in business records which again was used by limited groups.

By the time of King John's reign (1199-1216) it had become usual to make a written record of all official business. The records were written by clerks of the courts, by professional writers called scriveners, and in a few cases by private correspondents. By 1357 the professional

PARADIGM OF ALPHABETS

Set Chancery.		Common Chancery.		Court Hand		Secretary (Stuart Period)	

A general Alphabet of the Old Law Hands.

ALPHABETS from A. Wright's *Court Hand Restored* (5th ed., 1818, plates 18, 19), illustrating a variety of forms of letters, mainly but not entirely from 16th and 17th century Legal and Chancery hands.

handwriters of London had formed a gild known as The Scriveners' Company of London. These men called themselves "Writers of the Court Letter," and this description gave rise to the name of their type of handwriting as *Court Hand* in contrast with the *Book Hand* and *Text Hand*.

It must not be thought that the name *Court Hand* covers one style. In various courts in the country and at various times there were differences and changes in style to meet the requirements of the writers and the records they compiled so that a variety of *Court Hands* is to be found. Before the 16th century the highly skilled writers in the Chancery Court had developed a finer form of writing known as *Chancery Hand*, while the Exchequer Court had developed no less than three *Exchequer Hands* which were known as *King's Remembrancer's Hand*, *Lord Treasurer's Remembrancer's Hand*, and *Pipe Office Hand*.

The *Legal Hands* originated in the Royal Courts but it became common for these hands to be used outside the court records in documents made by lawyers and their clerks and by business men. Most manuscripts dating before 1500 are usually written in one form or another of *Court Hand*, and this type of old English handwriting was in use in official circles down into the 17th and 18th centuries. By the 18th century, the meaning of the term *Court Hand* had become restricted to mean the *Legal Hands*.

The New Learning or Renaissance was responsible for a greater demand for written records in a hand that could be read easily and written quickly. This new style, appearing as early as the middle of the 14th century, began as a mixture of earlier text hands but was more flowing and quicker to write, while at the same time it retained sufficient dignity that it could be used for professional purposes. It was known as *Bastard Hand* or *Bastard Secretary Hand*, and out of the latter other *Secretary Hands* developed.

In the 15th century there developed, first among Italian writers, another style of handwriting which was quicker to write and more cursive and became known as *Italic Hand*. Even though educated men and professional writers learned to use the *Italic Hand*, the various *Secretary Hands* remained popular with the professional writers. As time went on, writers began to mix *Court Hands*, *Secretary Hands*, and *Italic Hands*. Manuscripts will be found written basically in *Secretary Hand* but with important words or quotations distinguished by *Italic Hand*. It is from this dual use that the practice developed of using italics for emphasis in printed books.

Eventually the *English Round Hand* which is used today evolved from these types, as it did so adopting to a great degree the easier read, quicker written Italic form.

Until the introduction in about 1831 of fine steel pen points flexible enough to use in writing the *Round Hand*, there was no substitute for the quill pen.

For the record searcher there are no serious handwriting difficulties back to about 1700, but the beginner may find some difficult writing and abbreviations because the older form of handwriting did not immediately die out when the *Round Hand* came into use.

(1) Bastard Hand: c. 1432

A A B C D D E E F G H J K L M N O P Q R S T V W X

z

a b c č d đ e f e ğ hi i j k l l m n n o p q r r r r s s š ſ ſſ ſſ ft u v w x y z

bȝ q̃d

ħ pp pp ꝑ ꝑ ꝑꝑⁱ ꝝ ꝛ ꝺ qȝ ꝯ

nēci cõn cõ cõ et et

(2) Bastard Hand: 1571

a a b b c c c d d e e f ft g g h h i J J k k l m n o o

p p q q r r ſ š ſſ t tt u u v w w x y y z z et et et .

(3) *Fifteenth–Century Set Hand: temp.* Henry VII

A B C D E ff G H J K I M N O P R S T V V W X Y

a a bb c d de e f g gh hiij k ll m nno p p q r r r s ss ss ff tt v v w x y

ª ge ke H M P r ff tte lĩ ñ đ pᵉ

(4) *Fifteenth–Century Set Hand changing to Secretary:* 1539

a b c d e ff g h i j l m in imi un^9 o

z x w v tt ff ff ss ss r r ßß pi ßß ßß pi p p pi p

(5) *Secretary Hand: 1571*

a b c d e f g h i k l m n o p q r ſ t u x. y z et ſt w ꝭ.

(6) *Printed Secretary Hand: 1600*

A B C D ff J L M N O Q R S T

a b ꝑ c dr de eẽ f ff gh i k ll mnoop q re re r s ff fh ft th u v w x y z

(7) Secretary Hand: 1637

A   A O G Q T S   C E F J ff

N   N M V W V   P P R R B

B D D I L K H   H X Y Z Z

a b c d d e e f f g h i k l l m n o p   q r r ſt s t v u w x y z

(8) Engrossing Secretary Hand: 1658

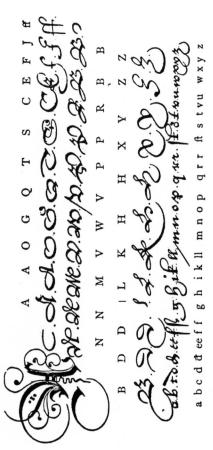

A a b c d d e e f f g h i k l ll m n o p q r f s ſt v u w x y z

(9) Sloped Secretary Hand: 1663 (but written much earlier)

A B C D E F F G   H J K L M N O P P

Q R S T V V W   W X Y Z A   B C D E F

A a b c d e e f g h t h i k l m n o p p q   r r f s s t v u w x y y z   et

(10) and (11) *Mixed Hands (Round-hand): c. 1670*

A a b c c d d e e f f g h h h i ij k k l all m n

N n o p p q q r r s fs st v v u w w x y y z z ꝝ

A a b c c d d e f g g h i k l m n o p q r s t v u w x y z

(12) *Chancery Hand:* 1571

A a a   B   b ƀ   C c c̄   D   đ   dđ   E   e   ee

ff   f̄   f̃   G   g̃   gg̃   H   hħ   h   J   i   J   ƙ   ƙ   ƙ

l   ħ   l   M   m   m̃   N   n   nñ   O   o   oo   o

P   p   p   P   pp   Q   q   q   R   r   r   S   s   ſs

T   t̃   t   v   v   w   u   x   x   y   y   z   z   9 .

(13) *Chancery Hand:* 1618

A a a B b b C c cc   D d đ   E e ee   ff   f f   ~

G g gh h h J i ij k k ƙ l ħ l M m mm

N n n O o oo P p pp Q q q R r r r R S s

ſ ſt T t tt   v u v u u   w w   x x   y y   z z   9

(14) *Chancery Capitals:* 1580

A B C D   E ff   G H J K l M   N O P   Q R S   T V W X Y Z

(15) *King's Remembrancer's Hand:* 1572

A B C CDD E ff G H J K l M N O P Q R S T V W X

a a b c d e e f g h ij k l m ni o p q r r ∫ s ct v w x y

~ ꝛ ᵃ te đ ll ñ p ꝑ ꝑꝛ r̄ ff ⁹

(16) *Pipe Office Hand:* 1592

A BCD E ff G H J K l M N O P R S T W X

a b c de f g h ij k l m n n o o p q r r sf ff t v vw x y z

ꝺ đ k u͂ ñ p ꝑ s͂ t͂ x͂

(17) Legal: 1571

P A A A a a a B B B b b b c C C c ct c̃

D D d d d d E e e e ff f G G g g̃ H h J J i

k k l H M M m nñ N N n nñ O O o oo o o P

P P P P Q Q q q R R r̃ r̃ S s s̃ ff

T T T t tt V V V v v u W W x x y y z z Et Et ʒ

(18) Small Legal: 1663 (but written much earlier)

A A a a a B Bb bb C Cc cc c D D dd dd E e ee e

ff ff f f G g gg ggh hh Ji iij jk k k k l l ll M M nuñ

miñ N inn inñ N O oo o P P pp p̃ Q Q q qñ d q R R r

S Sss ff T t tt v u v W W W x x x y y z z

(19) Large Legal: c. 1664

A a B b C c c D d dd E e ee ff ff G g gg

H J i ij i k l ll M m m̃ N n O o oo P p

P p P̃ Q q R r r S s st ff T t v u W x y z

(20) Medium Legal: c. 1664

P A a B b C c c̃ cc D D̃ d d̃ dd E e ee ff ff G g g̃ gg H J i ij i k k l ll M M̃ m m̃ m̃ N n ñ

O o oo P P̃ P̃ p p p̃ pf Q q R r r̃ or ʒ ea ʒ S s s̃ s̃ st ff T t t v u W x y z Et

A	$\mathcal{A}$ $\mathcal{SV}$
	a a
B	2ß $\mathcal{S}$
	ß B
C	$\ominus\ominus$
	† tc
D	$\vartheta\mathcal{d}$
	∂ $\mathcal{d}$
E	$\mathcal{EE}$
	℮ c
F	ff
	ſ f
G	$\mathcal{E}$ $\mathcal{G}$
	g y

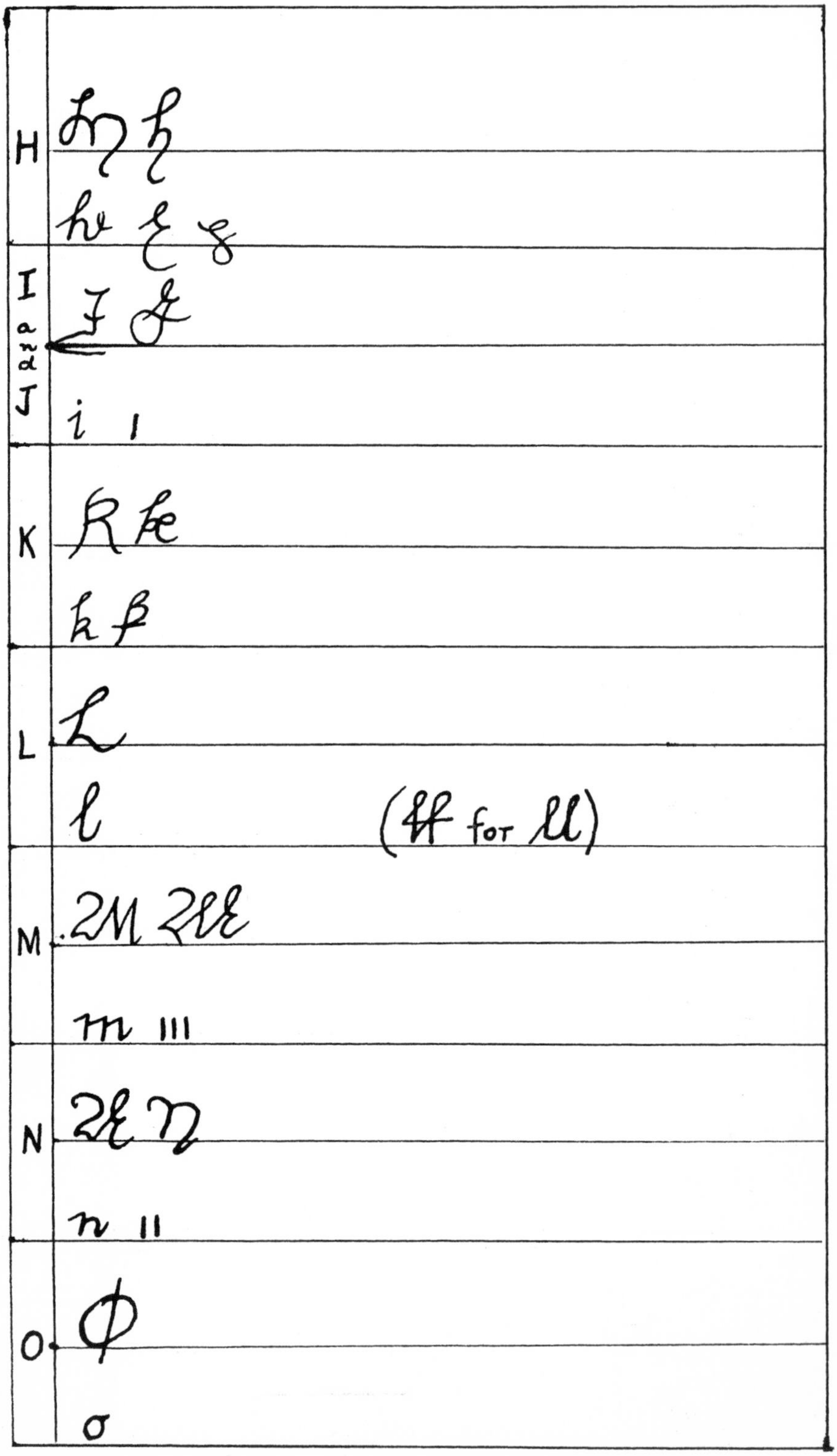
H
I and J
K
L
(ff for ll)
M
N
O

P	
Q	
R	
S	
sh	ss
st	
T	th
U a n d V	

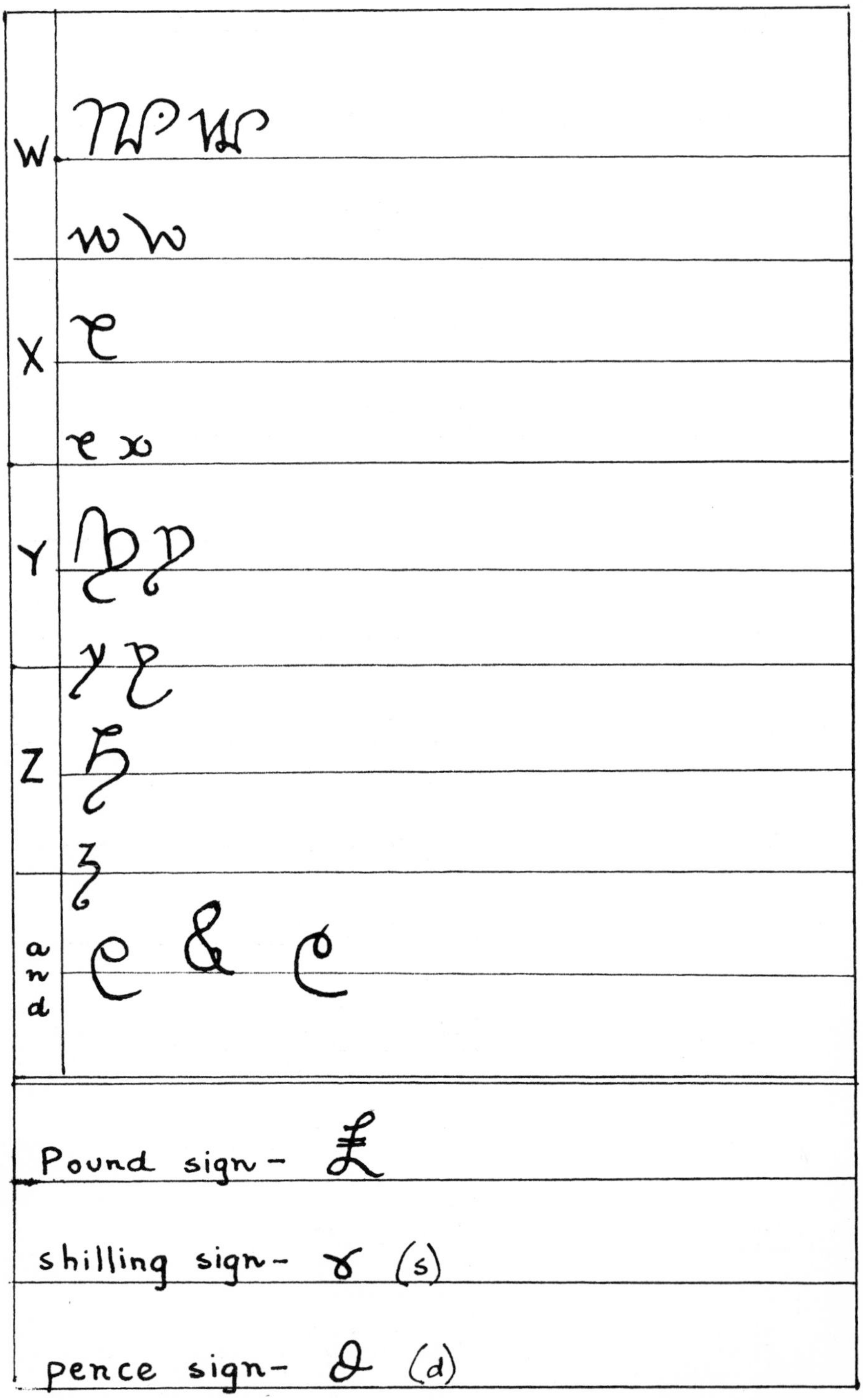
W
X
Y
Z
and
Pound sign -
shilling sign - (s)
pence sign - (d)

ROMAN		NUMERALS	
1	i or j	15	xv
2	ij	16	xvj
3	iij	17	xvij
4	iiij or jv or iv	18	xviij
5	v	19	xviiij or xjx or xix
6	vj	20	xx
7	vij	21	xxj
8	viij	22	xxij
9	viiij or jx or ix	23	xxiij
10	x (ꝯ)	24	xxiiij or xxjv or xxiv
11	xj	25	xxv
12	xij	26	xxvj
13	xiij	27	xxvij
14	xiiij or xjv or xiv	30	xxx

ROMAN   NUMERALS

L = 50	C = 100
D = 500	M = 1000
IↃ = 500	CIↃ = 1000

EXAMPLES

MCDXLV   = 1445

MCCCCXLV   = 1445

MCDLXV   = 1465

MDCXLV   = 1645

MDCCCXXI   =

MDXXVI   =

MONTHS AS NUMBERS AS FOUND IN OLD RECORDS

7^{ber} = September

8^{ber} = October

9^{ber} = November

10^{ber} = December

De Sepultis mense Octobris Anno Dom **1560** 12.

Isabella vx[or] Thome Talbot 2 ――――――― 1 die

Maria Scott ―――――――――――――― 10 die

Anna Flowle ――――――――――――― 26 die

Willmus Furfham 2 ―――――――――― 29 die

De Sepultis mensse Nouembris Anno Dom **1560**

Edmundus Singear 2 ―――――――― 3 die

Iacobus Groudfold et Iohana Braiell 2 9 die

Isabella Peate 2 ――――――――― eodem die

Rolandus Loy 2 ――――――――――― 13 die

Agnes vx[or] Willmi Loy 2 ――――――― 16 die

Willmus Flowle 2 ――――――――――― 19 die

Agnes vx[or] Mylome Loy 2 ――――――― 21 die

De Sepultis mense Decembris Anno Dom **1560**

Maria Tedder 2 ―――――――――――― 5 die

Emlia vx[or] Iarvis Mydleton 2 ―――――― 18 die

Isabella vx[or] Roger Harbru 2 ――――― 20 die

Agnes Conlor 2 ――――――――――― 22 die

Iohs Copper 2 ――――――――――― 23 die

De Sepultis mensse Januarij Anno Dom **1560**

Parish Register of Whalley, Lancs., England.

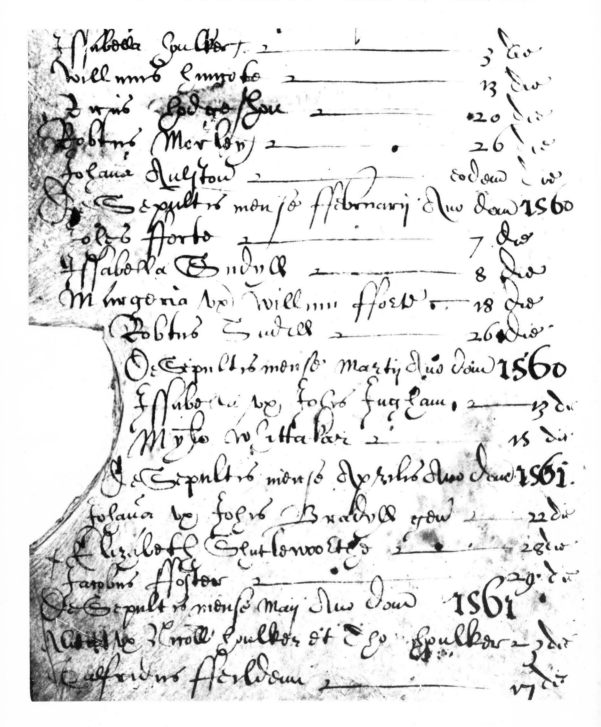

Parish Register of Whalley, Lancs., England.

DE SEPULTIS MENSE OCTOBRIS A'NO DOM' 1560.

Issabella ux' Thome Taulbot	1 die
Alicia Cowke	10 die
Aña ffowle	26 die
Wiłłmus Ingham	29 die

DE SEPULTIS MENSE NOUEMBRIS A'NO DOM' 1560.

Edwardus Saggar	3 die
Jacobus Greenefeld et Johaña Bradyll	9 die
Issabella Reade	eodem die
Nicolaus Hey	13 die
Agnes ux' Wiłłmi Hey	16 die
Wiłłmus ffowle	19 die
Agnes ux' Mylonis Hey	21 die

DE SEPULTIS MENSE DECEMBRIS A'NO DOM' 1560.

Alicia Seller	5 die
Cicilia ux' Jacobi Mydleton	18 die
Issabella ux' Rogeri Chatburne	20 die
Agnes Houlker	22 die
Jcħes Ropper	23 die

DE SEPULTIS MENSE JANUARIJ A'NO DOM' 1560.

Issabella Houlker	3 die
Wiłłmus Huncote	13 die
Riċus Hodgeshon	20 die
Robtus Morley	26 die
Jchaña Aulston	eodem die

DE SEPULTIS MENSE FFEBRUARIJ A'NO DOM' 1560.

Joħes fforte	7 die
Issabella Sudyll	8 die
Margeria ux' Wiłłmi fforte	18 die
Robtus Sudell	26 die

DE SEPULTIS MENSE MARTIJ A'NO DOM' 1560.

Issabella ux' Joħis Ingham	13 die
Mylo Whittakar	15 die

DE SEPULTIS MENSE APRILIS A'NO DOM' 1561.

Johaña ux' Joħis Bradyll gen'	22 die
Elizabeth Shutlewoorthe	28 die
Jacobus ffoster	29 die

DE SEPULTIS MENSE MAIJ A'NO DOM' 1561.

Alicia ux' Nicoł Houlker et Tho: Houlker	3 die
Galfridus ffeildenn	17 die

Oː Sepultis mensis July Ano Dom̄ 1561   125

Carolus Stow   2   8 do

Margreta vx Gulielmi Dobson   2   23 do

Margeria vx Robti Cogelton   2   27 do

Oː Sepultis mensis Augusti Ano Dom̄ 1561

Isabella Oghtbrowe   2   9 do

Ennas Goulden   2   10 do

Oː Sepultis mensis Septembris Ano Dom̄ 1561

Jacobus Brotherton   2   14 do

Jacobus Marton   2   16 do

Robtus Balston   2   20 do

Robtus Gutlewoortha   2   30 do

Oː Sepultis mensis Octobris Ano Dom̄ 1561

Josep Cogelton   2   1 do

Johana Stondon   2   7 do

Agneta vx Roberti Jacob   2   26 do

Oː Sepultis mensis Decembris Ano Dom̄ 1561

Jacob Wood   2   18 do

Agneta Utherows   2   19 do

Margreta Paull   2   26 do

? Alicia ? Corram 2 ——————————— 28 die

De Sepultis mensis Decembris Anno domini 1561

Margareta de .... 2 ———— 4 die

Johanna Watson ——————————— 19 die

De Sepultis mensis Januarij Anno domini 1561

Johanna ...... 2 ——————— 3 die

Robtus .... 2 ——————— 11 die

Robtus .... 2 ——————— 22 die

De Sepultis mensis Februarij Anno domini 1561

.... 2 ——————— 3 die

.... 2 ——————— 21 die

Margareta ..... 2 ——————— 24 die

De Sepultis mensis Martij Anno domini 1562

Alicia .. .. 2 ——— 27 die

De Sepultis mensis Aprilis Anno domini 1562

Margareta de .... ——— 4 die

Johanna ...... 2 ——————— 5 die

De Sepultis mensis May Anno domini 1562

.... 2 ——————— 7 die

De Sepultis mense Julij A'no Dom' 1561.

Nicolaus Lawe	8 die
Margreta ux' Humfryd' Dobson	23 die
Margeria ux' Roƀti Dogeshon	27 die

De Sepultis mense Augusti A'no Dom' 1561.

Issabella Chatburne	9 die
Thomas Houlden	10 die

De Sepultis mense Septembris A'no Dom' 1561.

Joħes Brotherton	14 die
Joħes Marter	16 die
Roƀtus Osbalston	20 die
Roƀtus Shutlewoorthe	30 die

De Sepultis mense Octobris A'no Dom' 1561.

Joħes Dogeshon	1 die
Johaña Stande[n] vi[dua]	7 die
Agneta ux' Xpoferi Cooke	26 die

De Sepultis mense Nouembris A'no Dom' 1561.

Joħes Wood	18 die
Agneta Clitherowe	19 die
Margareta Pollard	26 die
Elicia Norram	28 die

De Sepultis mense Decembris A'no Dom' 1561.

Margreta ux' Henrici Lawe	4 die
Johaña Watson	19 die

De Sepultis mense Januarij A'no Dom' 1561.

Jeaña Sudyll	3 die
Roƀtus Parkinson	11 die
Roƀtus Carryer	23 die

De Sepultis mense ffebruarij A'no Dom' 1561.

Nicolaus Heye	3 die
Ričus Shay	21 die
Margreta Chew	24 die

De Sepultis mense Martij A'no Dom' 1562.

Alicia ux' Ricardi Crombocke	27 die

De Sepultis mense Aprilis A'no Dom' 1562.

Margreta ux' Thome Cravyn	4 die
Johaña fforsha	5 die

De Sepultis mense Maij A'no Dom' 1562.

Joħes ffeilden	7 die

Will of William Moore, 1615,

Transcription of the Will shown on page 39.

William Moore of Rosemarket, 1615.

In the name of God Amen the sixt day of Februarii Anno Dmi 1615
I William Moore of the moore in the Pishe of Rosm'keett in the
county of Pembrocke yeoman beinge sicke in body but of good and
p'ffect mynd and memory laud and praise be unto Almightie God
Doe make my last will and testament in manor and fforme followinge
ffirst I bequeth my soule to almightie god my maker and my body
to be buried in the pish church of Rosm'kett Imprimis I Doe give
and bequeth to the pish church of Rosm'kett xxs to be paid when
the south sid is fully repaired Item I Doe give and bequeth unto
the Cathedrall church of St. Davis vid Item I Doe give and bequeth
unto Mary Phillips iis vid Item I Doe give and bequeth unto Jane
[cu]llum iis Item I Doe give and bequeth unto Mary the daughter
. . . (etc., etc.)

Suggestions to Instructor

1. Assign each student to fill each page of the alphabet provided
   in this chapter by copying each form of each letter at least
   five times.

2. Do not attempt to transcribe the pages from the Whalley registers but have the class point out all the abbrevations and the
   different signs used. (The Latin language used in Whalley registers is mentioned in Chapter 8.)

3. Give additional exercises on:

   Numerals

   Use of the letter "y"

   Use of the letters "f" and "s"

   Use of the minims "i" and "j"

CHAPTER FOUR

Progressive Reading and Writing Exercises

The letters of the alphabet having been studied, it is now essential to exercise in the joining of single letters to form words. It is recognized that in former times many scribes were apt to write the letters of a word singly, and not joined, but to place them close enough together to form a word. Sometimes the capital letter was not joined to the rest of the word. The majority of old handwriting, however, will be found with the letters joined in the same way as in modern hands.

People are more familiar with their own name than with any other words. In the space provided below, write your full name several times, using the letters on which you exercised in the previous chapter.

Listed below are words that include each capital and small letter of the alphabet. Write and re-write these words, using the letters exercised in the previous chapter.

Again

Barber

Circa

Dandy

Even

Fanfare

ffrancis

George

Hampshire

Illegitimate

Jeremiah

Major

Katharine

Sick

Lilly

Memorandum

Minim

Nanny

Naunton

Onion

Perfect

Upon

Appear

Quarto

Bequeath

Runner

Sisters

Moss

Trust

Unbaptised

Cause

Vestry

Serve

Walter

Swear

Xerxes

Executrix

Year

May

Zachariah

Ebenezer

The following words and phrases are reproductions from original documents. Write them several times as exact copies and then transcribe them to modern writing. If you wish to keep on practicing these examples, erase your writing or use additional paper. In case you have difficulty in transcribing correctly, the answers are to be found on page 52.

1. *John*

2. *Nothing*

3. *Smith*

4. *Hen*

5. *moore*

6. *some*

7. *Thomas*

8.

9.

10.

11.

12.

13.

14.

15. *declaringe*

16. *m{SUP}r{/SUP} A. Geffrey*

17. *earlbde*

18. *beed*

19. *restored*

20. *pronomncinge*

21. *goinge*

22. *keepe*

23. *God my maker*

24. *John yonnge*

25. *I doe giue*

26. *I William Ormond*

27. *Rich in bodie,*

28. *prisoundeme*

29. *and my debtes are*

30. *one hundred and xxx li in mony*

31.

32.

33.

34.

35.

36.

37. 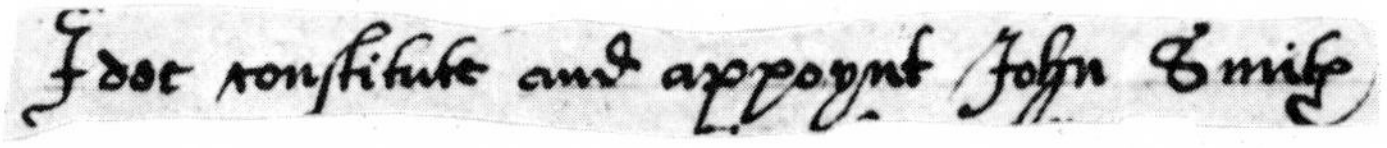

I doe constitute and appoynt John Smith

38. 

O Lorde Jesus Christ my saviour & redeemer,

39. 

40. *whome I doe make my whole executor to see my legacies paid*

41. *first I give & bequeath my soule vnto the hands of Almighty*

42. *vntill such time the said Allen come to the age of xxith yeares*

43. *Item I give vnto my sonne Ieutkin oueuious apeior of oxen*

44. *moveable and vnmoveable not given nor bequethed*

45. *to equally devided betvveen them both Item I doo give*

1. John   2. witnes   3. Smith   4. Item   5. Moore   6. come
7. Thomas   8. Kent   9. xx^th (20th)   10. goodes   11. ye (the)
12. iiij^d (four pence)   13. Pembrock (Pembroke)
14. xxxijs (32 shillings)   15. declaringe   16. my ffather (my Father)
17. lambes (lambs)   18. bees   19. costodie   20. pronouncinge
21. heiffer   22. keepe   23. god my maker   24. John Younge
25. I doe give   26. I Willam Ormond (I William Ormond)
27. sick in bodie   28. husbandman   29. and my debtes
30. One heyffer and xxxs in mony (1 heifer and 30 shillings in money)
31. my son David Ormond
32. Moriss Probert is to pay xxs (20 shillings)
33. Jenkin Millard   34. bequeath to my sister
35. when he is xxi^th yeares of age   36. at michaelmas Daie next
37. I doe constitute and appoynt John Smith
38. & unto Jesus Christ my Saviour & Redeemer
39. all my sheep that are in lodginge with John Marlow
40. whome I doe make my whole executor to see my legacies paid
41. ffirst I give & bequeath my soule into the handes of Almightie
42. untill such time the said Allen come to the age of xxi^he yeares
43. Item I give unto my son Jenkin Ormond a paier of oxen
44. moveable and unmoveable not given nor bequethed
45. be equally devided betwene them booth Item I dooe give

Suggestions to Instructor

The best way to learn to read old English hands is to write and rewrite them. Based on the general ability of the class, give whatever additional *writing* exercises are felt necessary.

Draw on the photographic reproductions in the text or on those in Volumes 1 and 2 of *Genealogical Research in England and Wales*. Libraries of universities and large cities may have books on handwriting, particularly those mentioned in the "Short List of Books" included at the end of Chapter 8.

Many libraries and record offices have reproduction services that might be used to obtain copies of old manuscripts or their microfilm copies. You could obtain such copies for close study and transcription by the class.

If the manuscript or microfilm copy as well as a transcription of a manuscript is in print, and both are available (either as books or photo-copies), it is worth obtaining both copies, having the class make transcripts, and then comparing these transcripts with the printed ones.

(Note the parish registers of Whalley in this book.)

CHAPTER FIVE

Examples of Secretary Hands

The Secretary Hands, one of which was known as Elizabethan Script, were widely used from the middle of the sixteenth century to the middle of the eighteenth century. This was the popular form used in parish registers, letters, and many types of documents other than legal documents. It was more popular than Court Hand because it was quicker and easier to write and to read. Reproductions of baptismal entries made during this period are shown in this chapter together with the transcriptions.

Baptismal entries from STANDISH PARISH REGISTER

Allice his wyfe . . .
the twenti third day of December 1677

Ann the Daughter of Hugh Heskin and
Ellizabeth his wyfe of Langtree was
baptized the twenti third day of December
1677   Humphry the son of Rich[ard] Nightingall of . . .
        Heath Charnocke was babt[ized] the 26 of Feb[ruary] 1677

Ellin the Daughter of Thomas Day and
Ellizabeth his wyfe of Adlington was
baptized the thirtinth day of January 1677

Ellizabeth the Daughter of Richard Guest
and Mary his wyfe of Standish was
baptized the thirtinth day of January 1677

Will[ia]m the sonne of Will[ia]m Bibby and Margaret
his wyfe of Worthington was baptized the
thirtith day of January 1677

Allice the Daughter of Edward Browne
and Mary his wyfe of the p[ar]ish of Eccleston
was baptized the third day of February 1677

Mary the Daughter of Allexander Chamberlen
and Clemence his wyfe of this towne was
baptized the third day of February 1677

Margery the Daughter of Thomas Clarkson
and Ellin his wyfe of Shevington was
baptized the third day of February 1677

Will[ia]m the sonne of Edward Tallior and Ellizabeth
his wife of Standish wood was baptized
the third day of February 1677

Maria filia Edwardi Chisenhale militis et Elizabethe
uxoris ejus nata 2° die Februarii 77 & baptizata
12° die Februarii 77

Austine the sonne of Tho[mas] Hatton
of Langtree was bapt[ized] the 30 of Dec[ember]

Allice his wyfe [...]

the twenti third day of December 1677

Ann the Daughter of Hugh Heskin and
Elizabeth his wyfe of Langtree was
baptized the twenti third day of December
1677 Humphrey son of Rich: Nightingall of [...]
Houth Charnock was baptized [...] of Feb: 1677

Ellin the Daughter of Thomas Fayand
Elizabeth his wyfe of Adlington was
baptized the thirtieth day of January 1677

Elizabeth the Daughter of Richard Guest
and Mary his wyfe of Standish was
baptized the thirtieth day of January 1677

Willm: the sonne of Willm: Wibby and Margaret
his wyfe of Worthington was baptized the
thirtieth day of January 1677

Allice the Daughter of Edward Browne
and Mary his wyfe of the pish of Eccleston
was baptized the third day of February 1677

Mary the Daughter of Alexander Chamber
and Ellenore his wyfe of this towne was
baptized the third day of February 1677

Margery the Daughter of Thomas Clarkson
and Ellin his wyfe of Shevington was
baptized the third day of February 1677

Willm: the sonne of Edward Tallior and Elizab
his wyfe of Standish wood was baptized
the third day of February 1677

Maria filia Edwardi Gerrineale militii et Elizabeth
uxoris ejus nata 2° die Februarij 77 & baptizata
i2°. die Februarij 77

John the sonne of Richard Crook and Allice
his wyfe of Coppull was baptized the
third of February 1677

Ellizabeth the Daughter of Edward Wholey
and Ellin his wyfe of Shevington was
baptized the third day of March 1677

Mary the Daughter of Richard Goodum
and Ellizabeth his wyfe of the p[ar]ish of
Eccleston was baptized the third day of March
1677

John the sonne of Robert Anderton and
Ellin his wyfe of Heath Charnock was
baptized the tenth day of March 1677

Timothy the sonne of James Farclough and
Ann his wyfe of Langtree was baptized
the fourtinth day of March 1677

Ellizabeth the Daughter of Will[ia]m Winnard
and Jane his wyfe of Shevington was
baptized the seventinth day of March
1677

Jane the Daughter of Peeter Hodson
and Margaret his wyfe of Adlington
was baptized the seventinth day of March
1677

Ellizabeth the daughter of Thomas
Halliwell and Ellin his wyfe of Standish
was baptized the twenti fourth day of
March 1677

Jane the Daughter of Will[ia]m Dalton of
Duxbury was baptized the twenti fourth
day of March 1677

Ellizabeth the Daughter of Roger Forster and
Dorathy his wyfe of Adlington was baptized
the seventh day of Aprill 1678

John the sonne of Robert Brooke and Ellis
his wyfe of Worrill was baptized the
third of February 1677

Elizabeth the Daughter of Edward Wholey
and Ellin his wyfe of Chorington was
baptized the third day of March 1677

Mary the Daughter of Richard Goodum
and Elizabeth his wyfe of the pish of
Eccleston was baptized the third day of March
1677 John the sonne of Robert Anderton and
Ellin his wyfe of Heath Charnock was
baptized the tenth day of March 1677

Timothy the sonne of James Sawbowrth and
Ann his wyfe of Ranstoto was baptized
the fourtinth day of March 1677

Elizabeth the Daughter of Willm Winnard
and Frew his wyfe of Chorington was
baptized the Seventink day of March
1677 Jane the Daughter of Peter Hodson
and Margaret his wyfe of Adlington
was baptized the seventinth of March
1677

Elizabeth the Daughter of Thomas
Hallizell and Ellin his wyfe of Standish
was baptized the twenti fourth day of
March 1677
Jane the Daughter of Willm Dalton of
Sudbury was baptized the twenti fourth
day of March 1677
Elizabeth the Daughter of Roger Forster and
Dorothy his wyfe of Adlington was baptized
the tenth day of Aprill 1678

Part of a page from STANDISH PARISH REGISTER, 1569

Henricus Greenhalghe Alicia Prescotte
xviiio die Septembris
Joh[ann]es Orrell   Anna Whalley
Gilbertus Baron   Margeria Halliwell
ixo die Octobris eiusd[em] Anni

Adamus Forster   Constancia Standishe
xviiio die octobris

Evanus Haidocke   Alicia Nightgall
xiiio die Novembris

Thomas Mirisone Alit[e]r Harisone Margeria Sclater
xxio Nove[m]bris

Jacobus Wigan, Johanna Vgnall [Ugnall]
quinto die Dece[m]bris

Thomas Dyconson, Katherina Vgnall [Ugnall]
ixo die Januarii

Radulphus Ashall, Margeria Nightgall
xvio die Januarii

Joh[ann]es Frythe   Clementia Walton
xixo die Januarii

Radulphus Standishe   Anna Forster
xxiio die Januarii

Suggestions to Instructor

Have the students study each example in this chapter, word by word, pointing out the letters with which they feel they may have difficulty.

Pay particular attention to those letters that look like some other, modern letters.

Emphasize the correct deciphering of capital letters as these will prove to be the most difficult in transcribing words.

Note the marriage of Thomas Mirisone. Use a Latin dictionary to find correct interpretation of this marriage.

Jacobus Greenhalghe Maria prestolle
    viij° die Septembris
Johes Croll Anna whalley
Gilbertus Baron Margeria hallivoll
    ix° die Octobris ... Ann
... forster Constancia Standige
    xviij° die octobris
... Haddocke Maria Nightgall
    xvij° die Novembris
Thomas Marijona Alit' hanston Margeria Orlator
    xij° die Novembris
Jacobus wigan, Johanna lynall,
    quinto die Decembris
Thomas Dyxonson Katherina lynall
    ix° die January
Radulphus Assall Margeria Nightgall
    xij° die January
Johes Arth... Clementia nalton
    xx° die January
Radulphus Standige Anna houston
    xxij° die January

CHAPTER SIX

Examples of Court Hands

The *Court Hands* were very elaborate and were principally used in preparing legal documents (hence they were often referred to as *Legal Hands*) during the sixteenth and seventeenth centuries. There are several differences between them and the *Secretary Hands* which was also in use at that time.

Here is an example taken from part of a Lancashire Quarter Sessions Roll dated 1642.

Quarter Sessions Roll

Sessions where shee was indyted and tryed accordinge to lawe beinge app[re]hended w[i]thin the same towne of Ormiskirke [*faded*] sent to the said House of Correcc[i]on or otherwise an attachm[en]t shalbee awarded ag[ains]t them to answer their contempte [*faded*] att the next Sessions of Peace here to bee houlden

Forasmuch as upon the informac[i]on of Will[ia]m Forth gent-[leman] Mayor of the towne and burrowe of Wigan divers of the A[lderme]n and bayliffes of the same towne and other inhabitants there that there are severall p[ar]cells of goods taken as is conceaved out of from and about the towne of Salford and brought into the same burrowe of Wigan and into some other places nere adioyninge by sundry p[er]sons conceaved that have not bought or obtayned the same in any lawfull way for the right owners thereof and prayeth the direction opinion and advise of this courte how and in what manner the same may bee restored unto the true owners thereof All w[hi]ch this courte takeing into due considerat[i]on doe conceave that aswell the said goods so taken & brought from Salford or any other place adiacent ought to bee stayed and seized upon as already they are or hereafter may bee found out and kept by the officers of those severall townes whereunto such goods are or hereafter shalbee brought or found out as after such p[er]sons or p[er]son as do or shall bringe or convey any such goods ought to bee taken notice of that as occasion may fall out they may bee sent for to answer the haveinge or keepeing of the same goods or any of them And this courte doth further declare that if any such p[er]son or p[er]sons as shalbee conceaved or charged to have brought in any such goods doe upon demand by any mayor bayliffe constable or other officer deny [*faded*] to bringe forth and give a iust accompt & p[ar]ticular of all and every such goods as shall in any such wise come unto their hands or deliver the same over into the hands of such said officer soe as the same may be duely and truely returned and redeliv[er]ed unto the right owner or owners upon due prooffe thereof made Then the Justices here p[re]sent doe offer and promise upon notice given to come over and take informat[i]ons therein and to bynd over or therein [*faded*] p[ro]ceede ag[ains]t such as shall bee delinquents according to lawe And this Courte doth desire and hopes that

Suggestions to Instructor

Have the students study each example word by word. Have them point out those words or letters which give them difficulty. These should be practiced in writing in order to achieve familiarity with them.

CHAPTER SEVEN

Examples of Italic Hand

All the modern forms of handwriting are individual versions of the *Italic* or *Italian Hand*, which began gradually replacing *Secretary Hands* for general use as early as the seventeenth century. Here are two examples of *Italic* handwriting. It will be noted that in the first one, dated 1716, the writer is still using a few *Secretary* and *Court Hand* letters.

The will of SARAH COWLEY (part) dated 1716

the sume of ten shillings Item I give unto Elizabeth tickle of Warington Sarah Lyon Ales Lyon Martha Cliffe Ellinor taylor and Mary Taylor every one the sume of five shillings item I give twenty shillings to be devided Amongest the poore in the neighbourhood item I give unto Joseph Gillibourn of windle Clarke and John Pottes of heendley Linen weuer [weaver] fiue [five] pounds betwixt them and whereas I the said Sarah Cowley do now stand seized and lawfully posesed of one mesuage or Tenement where on i now dwell and which i now occupy and poses containing by estimation six acres be the same more or less i do hereby will giue [give] and devise the same and euery [every] part and parcell thereof with the Appurtenances unto Joseph Gillibourn of windle in the County of Lanc[a]s[ter] afforesaid Cleark his heirs upon the several trusts uses Intents and purposes and chargeable as is here after mentioned Limitted expressed appointed and declared That is to say that he the said Joseph Gillibourn his heires shall and will Imediately from and after my death and decease satisfye pay and discharge forth and out off the Cleer yearly Rents Issues and proffits of the aboue [above] mentioned messuage and tenement with the appurtenances all the Residue and Remander of the proper and Just debts and Legazyes aboue [above] mentioned and funeral Expences of me the said Sarah Cowley which my Goods and personal Estate shall fall short to pay off and discharge in maner Aforesaid and from and after the payment of my debts Legazies and funerall Expences then it is further my will and mind and I do give and bequath the rest and remander of what I have either in goods or estate for the bringing up of poore persons children to the scools at St Elins and my mind and will is that when the monyes shall fall giuen [given] unto Mrs Naylor either at her mariage or death and likewise if there shall not be a decenting minister at the new chappel at St. Elins that then it shall both be aded to what I have and shall order for the bringing up of poore persons children to the scools for euer [ever] such as are not able to pay for the same themselues [themselves] and to find them with bookes as the horne booke the primer salter teastiment and the bible till they can read the bible and to have one when they go of and iff the proffits of the estate and monyes will do more then this then my mind and will is that the Remander shall be laide out in linins and clothes for

Will of Sarah Cowley, 1716.

Letter describing a voyage from the Isle of Man via Gambia
to Virginia with 130 slaves. (31 July 1752)

Virginne July ye 31

On Bord ye Ellizabeth in Rapahannack River in 1752
I Having this Oppertunity By William Dixon macks it My Bisness
to Lett My Dear hear from heir Own. We arived here ye 29 of
Do. after a fine Passige of 6 Weeks from Gambia With one hundred
and Thirty Slaves We have had a virre Good Voige as for the
Slaves Doing us any harm They Never So Much as atempted to Do
us any [harm] I Thank God for it I have had My health Virre Well.
I Cannot Give the River of Gambia a Bad Carracter as to health
the Virre few on Bord of Our Snow Can Say the Same we Buried 4
of our People there and Boath [*two words crossed out*] we and all
the Ships in the River [*had crossed out*] Was Virre Sickley this
Year and had Great Mortahty on Bord of them We Came from
there the 16 Day of June and we Left there the Casteltown Capten
Tindall from Lancaster he Could nott Saill When We Did he had
buried 4 hands and all the Rist was in a Virre bad State of health
We Sailed from the [*IS crossed out*] Island of Man the 2 Day of
March and we arived at Gambia ye 26 of Do. We have had fine
passigs so far, I Cannot Give the any account as Yett how Long
our Stay Will Be in this Country as Yett for We are Going up
the River to Sell Our Cargo I Writte to the the [*sic*] from Gambia
the 29 of March by the Cumberland Snow She Was for Sailling
in a few Days after ours I have not much more to Write at Prisant
But My Duty to parants and Love to Brothers and Sisters and
Service to [*error*] All Enquiring frinds So no more at Prisent from
thy Loving husband

 Thomas Harrison.

Letter from Virginia, 1752.

Here is a copy of a comparatively modern document. It will be noted that very few of the difficult older style letters are being used.

LETTER RE PETERLOO MASSACRE (part) 1819

Dear Sir,

Having this Day received from Lord Sidmouth the inclosed Letter by command of the Prince Regent requesting me to express to the Magistrates of the County Palatine of Lancaster who attended at Manchester on Monday last, the great satisfaction derived by his Royal Highness from their prompt decision & official Measures for the preservation of the public tranquility;

I take the Earliest Opportunity of forwarding to you (& requesting you will communicate to the other Gentlemen who acted with you upon the occasion alluded to) this full approbation of your's and their conduct, & of the Measures taken by you in the discharge of your Official Duty as Magistrates of this County

I have the Honor to be

Copperplate is a version of the Italic style developed by professional writing masters and usually used in official documents. Here is an example taken from part of a Surrender of Property, 1858. (Page 68)

Suggestions to Instructor

The *Italic Hands* present little difficulty. It is interesting to note, however, that individual writers carried letters over from Court and *Secretary Hands*. Have these letters pointed out and make sure that each class member can read every word of the examples.

Letter about the Peterloo Massacre, 1819.

To all to whom these Presents shall come David Smith of New Park Road Clapham Park Esquire Anna Algehr Smith of the same place Spinster George Bayly of Lansdown Crescent Notting Hill Esquire James Dudgeon Bayly of George Yard Lombard Street Stationer John Lambert of the New Finchley Road Esquire and William Smith Boyd of 2 Moorgate Street City of London Esquire Send Greeting Whereas the messuage or tenement and hereditaments hereinafter described are with other hereditaments comprised in and demised by an Indenture of Lease bearing date the fourteenth day of March One thousand seven hundred and eighty four made between Mary Windham Bowyer Widow and Joseph Windham Esquire of the first part and William Smith Gentleman of the other part for a term of Seventy five years from the twenty fifth day of March One thousand seven hundred and eighty four and the same premises are now vested in and held by the above named parties or some of them for the residue of the said term

Surrender of property, 1858.

CHAPTER 8

Some Notes on Reading Entries Written In Latin[1]

Although the interpretation of many Latin documents will require a thorough knowledge of Latin, it is possible for most people to make a correct interpretation of Latin entries in parish registers provided that certain basic rules of Latin are known. It is foolhardy to guess the English translation, because what may seem obvious may not be a correct interpretation.

As we know from our school days, the name of a person, place or thing is a *noun*. In Latin each noun has a basic spelling, known as the base or stem of the word, to which are added various terminations. Latin nouns are divided into five groups according to the type of endings employed, and these five groupings are known as declensions. In each declension the final letters of the noun are changed to indicate distinctly what is meant. These various forms of a Latin noun are called *cases*. A noun is thus declined to indicate that it is the subject or the object of the verb, or to indicate possession, and so on, as well as to indicate singular or plural. For our purpose let us consider five cases found in Latin:

	Latin	**English**
1. The *nominative* case is used as the subject of the sentence:	*Robertus*	Robert
2. The *genitive* case indicates possession or the English preposition *of:*	*Roberti*	of Robert (or Robert's)
3. The *dative* case indicates the person indirectly affected by the action of the verb:	*Roberto*	to or from Robert
4. The *accusative* case indicates the direct object of the action of the verb or the person directly affected:	*Robertum*	Jane married Robert
5. The *ablative* case modifies the verb by indicating t h e means *(by what)*, the manner *(how)*, the place *(which)*, the time *(when)*, or the agency *(by whom)*.	*Roberto*	by Robert

As we would expect from the explanation already given, the stem of the noun is unchangeable — *Robert*, only the endings vary.

---

[1]Further study for those whose knowledge of Latin is weak would be the excellent text-book by Eileen A. Gooder, *Latin for Local History* (London: Longmans, Green & Co., 1961), price $3.00.

Sometimes a Latin preposition will be used in conjunction with the noun: e.g., *ab* = by or from; *cum* = with; *de* and *ex* = from; *in* = in or on.

In parish registers most female given names are first declension nouns; the majority of male given names are in the second declension while a few are in the third declension. The recognition of these forms is further simplified by the fact that the dative and accusative cases and the plural forms of nouns are rarely seen in parish registers.

Note the four given names Henry, Robert, Alice, and Mary:

Nominative (Subject)	Henricus	Robertus	Alicia	Maria
Genitive (Possessive)	Henrici	Roberti	Aliciae	Mariae or Marie
Accusative (Object)	Henricum	Robertum	Aliciam	Mariam
Ablative (By, with, from)	Henrico	Roberto	Alicia	Maria

This entry from a parish register illustrates the point:

> *Henrici et Aliciae fil: Robertus Smith*

A novice unaware of Latin word forms might translate this to read:

> *Henry and Alice children of Robert Smith*

This hopelessly incorrect translation does not take into consideration that "Henrici" and "Aliciae" mean "of Henry" and "of Alice," and that Robertus is the subject of the sentence; hence the entry reads:

> *Robert Smith son of Henry and Alice*

The following illustrates entries that might be found in the same parish register[2] but where different forms of nouns were used according to the method of entry followed by the parish clerk:

Nominative form for the groom and bride: Robertus Woolfall et Alicia Parr [were married].

Genitive form for the groom and bride: [The marriage of] Roberti Woolfall et Aliciae Parr.

Nominative form for the *groom* but accusative form for the *bride*:   Robertus Woolfall [married] Aliciam Arnold.

---

[2]Examples of this nature will be found in *The Parish Registers of Sefton, Lancs.*, Lancashire Parish Register Society, vol. 86:[1947]).

A list of many Latin given names showing their nominative, genitive, and ablative forms is given, commencing at page 87. Common female given names which occur in the first declension and have the final ending of -a (as in Maria) are not included, since they follow the same form as Mary — *Maria, Mariae, Maria,* and can easily be recognized. Given names found in old documents are often badly spelled, such as "Bricheta" (*Brigitta*), "Gawtherus" (*Galterus*), and "Gilbartus" (*Gilebertus*). To include such as these would not only mislead but also create an endless listing. It has, therefore, been necessary to limit the list to principal spellings.

The following exercise in reading entries is from a printed parish register covering an early period. These are chosen to bring out points with which each researcher will need to be familiar. Reference will need to be made to the list of Latin terms and their meanings; to the explanations of abbreviations; and to Latin numerals. Work out the correct English version of these entries before turning to the answers which follow.

EXERCISE IN READING ENTRIES
IN EARLY PARISH REGISTERS

Weddinges 1585
July. Xpofer Walker & Alice Murton the xviijth day

Weddinges 1587
August. Joħes P'ker et Agnes Scholes vicesimo die

1590 Christenings
June
    Gilbtus filius Michaelis Waide et Willus filius Ricĩ Male vicesimo
       primo die

November
    Isabella filia iligitima Ricĩ Harrison vicesimo primo die
December. Agneta filia Edmundi Nicson sexto die
    Francisca filia Niчħis Coward eodem die
    Thomas filius Henrici Wilson decimo quinto die
    Lawrencius filius Niчħi Crowswell suprius vicesimo primo die,
       mothers name ys Ane Wilson
Januarie. Elizabetha filia Thome Johnson tercio die
    Matheus filius Willmi Powell decimo die

1592 Christenings
September. Robtus filius Robti Fyrth tercio die
October
    Willus filius Willmi Pollett et Agnes filia Stephani Calu'ley vicesimo
       septimo die

March
    Willmus filius Tho: Ou'ende et Edwardus filius Hugonis septimo die

1582 Burialls
William Westermã the xxijth day

1587 Burialls
December
    Anna uxor Jacobi Stringfield septimo die
    Elizabetha filia Edmundi Lumbie defuncti undecimo die
    Margareta Dobson vidua duodecimo die
Januariẽ
    Ricũs Tompson ultimo die

1596 Burialls
December
    Eliz: filia Lawrencij Butterfeld ultimo die
Januarie. Ricũs Burton, als Caruer 10 die
    Jeneta ux. Caroli Houltes 24 die

1605 Burialls
Januarij
    Alicia Oates uxor Richardi Oates sepulta fuit duodecimo die

Answers and explanations to exercise in reading early parish registers.

Weddings 1585.
July. Christopher Walker and Alice Murton the 18th day.

The X in Xpofer is the same as the X in Xmas (Christmas).

Weddings 1587.
August. John Parker and Agnes Scholes 20th day.

John is abbreviated Latin. Parker is only determined by the fact that
there is an abbreviation mark and that other entries relating to this couple
clearly show the name to be Parker. Otherwise the surname could have
been Packer, Picker, Pecker, etc.

1590 Christenings
June. Gilbert son of Michael Waide and William son of Richard Male 21st
    day.

These are *two* christening entries written on the same line by the parish
clerk. Notice that both the given names of the boys are in abbreviated
Latin but have no abbreviation signs.

November. Isabella illegitimate daughter of Richard Harrison the 21st day.

December. Agnes daughter of Edmund Nicson (Nixon) 6th day.

    Frances daughter of Nicholas Coward the same day.

To obtain the date of christening reference will need to be made to the date
of the preceding entry. In this instance it would be the sixth day.

    Thomas son of Henry Wilson 15th day.

Lawrence spurious [i.e., illegitimate] son of Nicholas Crowswell 21st day, mother's name is Anne Wilson.

January. Elizabeth daughter of Thomas Johnson third day.

Matthew son of William Powell tenth day.

1592 Christenings.
September. Robert son of Robert Fyrth (Firth) third day.

Note the *nominative* and *genitive* endings in the given name Robert.

October. William son of William Pollett and Agnes daughter of Stephen Calverley 27th day.

This is another entry containing two christenings. In the surname Calverley note that it is abbreviated in the original and the letter 'u' is used instead of the letter 'v'. The letters were used interchangeably in those days, usually to indicate 'v'.

March. William son of Thomas Overend and Edward son of Hugh 7th day.

Note especially the surname Overend. The original register used the same arrangement as for Calverley. This is another entry containing two christenings but the surname for the second entry was not recorded in the register.

1582 Burials. William Westerman the 22nd day.

In this entry the abbreviations are obvious. In other abbreviated entries the correct translation is not so obvious.

1587 Burials.
December. Anna wife of [James or] Jacob Stringfield 7th day.

As Jacob in Latin can mean either James or Jacob in English this is the way the entry must be interpreted unless further evidence will clearly define the given name as one or the other.

Elizabeth daughter of Edmund Lumbie, deceased, 11th day.

Edmund and Edward are often interchangeable at this period of time. The surname is undoubtedly Lumb given in Latin as Lumbie, and it would be difficult to arrive at Lumb unless the researcher was familiar with the locality surnames or had access to later registers written in English. If this was a parish in which ancestors were living the person performing the research would have familiarized himself with the surnames existing in the parish in the later, more readable registers. The word "defuncti" is genitive and therefore relates to Edmund Lumb, who is dead at the time of his daughter's christening.

Margaret Dobson, widow, 12th day.

January. Richard Thompson 31st day.

"Ultimo die" meaning *the last day*. In this case it is January, therefore the date of burial will be the 31st.

1596 Burials.

December. Elizabeth or Eliza daughter of Lawrence Butterfield 31st day.

The abbreviation of the child's given name could be either Eliza or Elizabeth, but is most likely Elizabeth.

January. Richard Burton or Carver 10th day.

'als' is an abbreviation of 'alias' which is translated to 'or'. Note the use of the letter 'u' in the surname Carver.

Janet wife of Charles Holt 24th day.

1605 Burials.

January. Alice Oates wife of Richard Oates was buried 12th day.

Ux. is the common abbreviation used for uxoris (wife).

Suggestions to Instructor

1. Point out how easy it is to arrive at a completely erroneous version of an entry written in Latin unless the Latin word endings are correctly understood. Prepare additional examples if you think them necessary. See examples from Whalley parish registers in Chapter 3.

2. Using all the reference material in this chapter, devise entries as they would appear in parish registers and have the class translate them. Make extensive use of the reference material provided in the chapter. Take an extra lesson on this.

The following exercise involves the translation of six pages of an original parish register. The correct interpretation is given in square brackets after each entry.

WEDDINGES 1582

September. Thomas Flynt and Agnes Duffon the ixth day
[Thomas Flynt (Flint) and Agnes Duffon the 9th day]

Myles Abbot and Elizabeth Clarebrough the xith day
[Myles Abbot and Elizabeth Clarebrough the 11th day]

1582 CHRISTENIN[GS]

August.   Elizabeth Townend the xxiith day
[Elizabeth Townend the 22nd day]

September.   George Wrooe the ixth day
[George Wrooe (Wroe or Roe) the 9th day]

Richard Robinson the ixth day
[Richard Robinson the 9th day]

Tho: Franke the xvith day
[Thomas Franke the 16th day]

Elizabeth Fether the xxiith day
[Elizabeth Fether (Feather) the 22nd day]

Joan Hogdin the xxiith day
[Joan Hogdin (Ogden) the 22nd day]

Tho: Walker the xxiiith day
[Thomas Walker the 23rd day]

1582 BURIALLS

August.   Beatrix Stanege the xxvth day
[Beatrix Stanege (Beatrice Standage) the 25th day]

September.   Thomas Wright the iith day
[Thomas Wright the 2nd day]

Agnes Haylye the xxxth day
[Agnes Haylye (Haley) the 30th day]

1582

August

Weddinges	Christenn	Burialls
	Elizabeth Townend the xxv th day	Beatrix Stannge the xxvi th day

September 1582

Wedd	Christenn	Burialls
Thomas Abbot and Agnes Dufton the i th day	George Wroe the i th day	Thomas wright the vi th day
Myles Abbot and Elizabeth Marchbrony the xi th day	Richard Robinson the vi th day	Agnes Daulbye the xxx th day
	Tho: ffrauke the xxi th day	
	Elizabeth fflethe the xxvi th day	
	Joan heydin the xxvi th day	
	Tho: walkes the xxvi th day	

1582 WEDD[INGS]

Januarie.   Willia Woode & Elizabeth Powell the xxixth day
[William Woode (Wood) and Elizabeth Powell the 29th day]

1582 CHRISTENINGES

December.   Tho: Collinson the xxiith day
                    [Thomas Collinson the 21st day]

Januarie.   Agnes Flancell the vith day
                      [Agnes Flancell the 6th day]

                        Ane Dawson the xiiith day
                      [Anne Dawson the 13th day]

                        Elline Ingle the xvth day
                       [Ellen Ingle the 15th day]

                      Alis Blackburne the xxvith day
          [Alice Blackburne (Blackburn) the 26th day]

                      Anthonie Becke the xxviith day
          [Anthony Becke (Beck) the 27th day]

1582 BURIALLS

                     John Kitchinman the xxviiith day
                    [John Kitchinman the 28th day]

December.   William Lynley the iith day
                    [William Lynley the 2nd day]

                        Jayne Holmes the iiiith day
                       [Jane Holmes the 4th day]

                        Clarke wife the xxiith day
          [Clarke wife the 21st day (meaning the wife of Mr. Clarke)]

                      Thomas Chambers the xxvith day
                     [Thomas Chambers the 26th day]

Januarie.   James Chamber the iiiith day
                    [James Chamber(s) the 3rd day]

                      Dorathie Croft the viith day
                      [Dorothy Croft the 7th day]

                        Barbarie More the xvth day
                      [Barbara More the 15th day]

                        Willia Flancell the xixth day
                    [William Flancell the 19th day]

                      Emmot Wormall the xxixth day
                      [Emmot Wormall the 29th day]

1582

december

Wedd:	Christenings	Buriالls
	Tho: Tollinson the xxjth day	Willia Lynley the ixth day
		Jayne Holmes the injth day
		Clarke wife the xxjth day
		Thomas Chambers the xxxth day

John Kitchinman the xxviith day

1582

Januarie

Wedd	Christem	Buriالls
	Agnes Flawell the vjth day	James Chambe this injth day
	Anne dawson the xvijth day	Dorathie Frost the xvjth day
Willia wedde 3 Elizabeth Powell the xxixth day	Anne Fuyle the xxth day	Barbarie More the xxth day
	Alis Blackburne the xxvijth day	willia Flawell the xxjth day
	Antonie Porter the xxvijth day	Ennot wormall the xxvijth day

WEDD[INGES] 1585

Februarie.   Bryan Wilson & Jennett Tattersall the xiiith day
[Bryan Wilson and Jennet Tattersall the 13th day]

Willia Shawe & Margrett Baraclough the same day
[William Shawe (Shaw) and Margaret Baraclough the same day
(13th)]

1585 CH
[1585 CHRISTENING]

Februarie.   Richard Carter the vth day
[Richard Carter the 5th day]

John the sone of Willia Gloue' the vith day
[John son of William Glover the 6th day]

Franciscus filius Willmi Dobson de Carleton the xijth
[Francis son of William Dobson of Carleton the 12th]

Anna filia Edward Agland the xiith day
[Ann (or Anna) dau. of Edward Agland the 12th day]

Anthonius filius Gilbti Longbothome the 24th day
[Anthony son of Gilbert Longbottom the 24th day]

1585 BURIALLS

Februarie.   [blank] Bedforth the vth day
[Bedforth (alternative spelling for Bedford) the 5th day]

Richard Carter the viith day
[Richard Carter the 7th day]

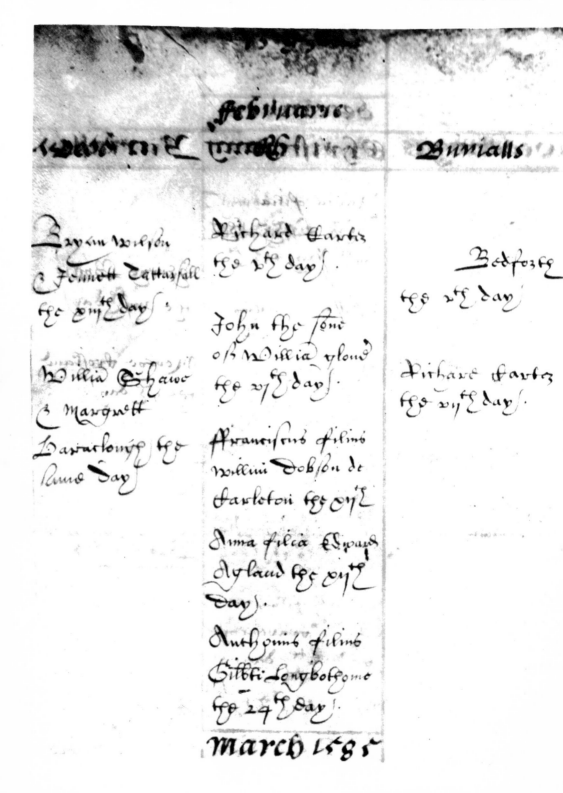

WEDDINGES 1588

August.   Xpofer Roydes and Elizabeth Scofeld the 4th day
[Christopher Roydes (Rhodes) and Elizabeth Scofeld (Schofield)
the 4th day]

September.   Franciscus Dobso et Agnes Hornbie primo die
[Francis Dobson and Agnes Hornbie (Hornby) 1st day]

Xpoferus Hopton et Agnes Hargraue decimo quinto die
[Christopher Hopton and Agnes Hargrave 15th day]

1588 CHRISTENINGS

August.   Willus filius Willmi More decimo octavo die
[William son of William More 18th day]

Thomas Haworth vicesimo quarto die
[Thomas Haworth 24th day]

September.   Suzanna filia Mathei Leigh gen' octauo die
[Suzanna dau. of Matthew Leigh, gentleman, 8th day]

Gilbtus filius Gilbti Walker de Carleton vicesimo sexto die
[Gilbert son of Gilbert Walker of Carleton, 26th day]

Suzanna filia Jacobi Dobson iunior' vicesimo nono die
[Suzanna dau. of James (or Jacob) Dobson, Junior, 29th day]

1588 BURIALLS

August.   Robtus Calu'ley sexto die
[Robert Calverley 6th day]

Johes Seele nono die
[John Seele 9th day]

Georgius Mylner undecimo die
[George Mylner 11th day]

Jana Browne duodecimo die
[Jane Browne 12th day]

Alicia Cockell widow decimo octavo die
[Alice Cockell widow, 18th day]

September.   Agnes P'ker quarto die
[Agnes Parker 4th day]

Isabell Wriglesforth decimo quinto die
[Isabel Wriglesforth 15th day]

Anna Cliffe decimo septimo die
[Ann (or Anna) Cliffe 17th day]

[Handwritten parish register facsimile, partially legible]

1588

August

Weddings	Christenings	Burialls
Xpofer ffoydes and Elizabeth Greford the 4ᵉ day.	Willus filius Willmi More decimo octavo die.	Robert Calidleys septo die.
	Thomas Hawoth vicesimo quarto die.	John Steele nono die.
		Georgius my luck vndecimo die.
		Jana Browne Duodecimo die.

1588

September

Wedd:	Christenings	Burialls
Francistus dobso et Agnes Stenubic prima die.	Suzanna filia Mather Longe god octavo die.	Agnes pke quarto die.
	Gilbertus filius Gilbt Walker de Sarkston vicesimo septo die.	Isabell wrughsforth Decimo quinto die.
Xpoforus Hopton et Agnes Hargrave Decimo quinto die	Suzanna filia Jacobi Dobson inmod vicesimononono die.	Anna Clifte Decimo septimo die.
		Alicia Berkell widow Decimo octavo die.

ADDITIONAL CHRISTENINGS:

[1588]   Jennet filia Nichi Royd' decimo nono
[Jennet dau. of Nicholas Royd (could be Rhodes or might be an
abbreviation for Roydhouse) 19th (day)]

Henricus Wright vicesimo secundo die
[Henry Wright 22nd day]

Thomas filius Willmi Lockwood xxviiit die
[Thomas son of William Lockwood 28th day]

ADDITIONAL BURIAL:

[1588]   Margareta Postlewhaite vicesimo tercio die
[Margaret Postlewhaite 23rd day]

WEDDINGES [1588]

[Nouember.] Thomas Ou'end et Katherina Robinson decimo septimo die
[Thomas Overend and Catherine Robinson 17th day]

Tho: Moxon et Joan Stanfeild decimo quarto die
[Thomas Moxon and Joan Stanfeild (Stansfield) 14th day]

Joħes Broke vica' de Camsill et Anna Cockell vicesimo sexto die
[John Broke (Brook) vicar of Camsill (Campsall) and Ann
(or Anna) Cockell 26th day]

December.   Roƀtus Wilson et Alicia Smyth primo die
[Robert Wilson and Alice Smyth (Smith) 1st day]

Roƀtus Fosarde et Anna Townend 3cio die
[Robert Fosarde and Ann (or Anna) Townend 3rd day]

Tho: Browkhouse et Jennett Bussie, Roƀtus Clarke et Margareta
[Thomas Browkhouse (Brookhouse) and Jennet Bussie, Robert
Clarke and Margaret

P'ker, Georgius Benton et Agnes Dann decimo die
Parker, George Benton and Agnes Danson 10th day]

[1588] CHRISTENINGES

[Nouember.]   Roƀtus filius Wiłłmi Webster de Rothwell primo die
[November. Robert son of William Webster of Rothwell 1st day]

Alicia Collinson nono die
[Alice Collinson 9th day]

[blank] filia Joħis Hyndle decimo die
[daughter of John Hyndle (Hindle) 10th day]

Anna filia Rĩci Wright decimo septimo die
[Ann (or Anna) dau. of Richard Wright 17th day]

December.   Anna filia Joħĩs Spencer primo die
[Ann (or Anna) dau. of John Spencer 1st day]

Maria filia Joħis Lynley secundo die
[Maria (or Mary) dau. of John Lynley (Linley) 2nd day]

Agnes filia Thomae Swifte quarto die
[Agnes dau. of Thomas Swifte 4th day]

Isabella filia Wiłłmi Forman decimo quarto die
[Isabella dau. of William Forman 14th day]

Maria filia Thome Heptenstall et Tho: filius Jacobi Dobson
de Carleton spurius 15to die
[Maria (or Mary) dau. of Thomas Heptenstall and Thomas son
of James (or Jacob) Dobson of Carleton, spurious, 15th day]

Ricũs filius Robti
[Richard son of Robert]

[1588] BURIALLS

November.   Anthonius Robinson tercio die
[Anthony Robinson 3rd day]

Robtus Webster filius Thome Webster decimo quarto die
[Robert Webster son of Thomas Webster 14th day]

December.   Francis Dobson's childe 7 die
[Francis Dobson's child 7th day]

Agnes ux' p'd'ci Francisci Dobson octavo die
[Agnes wife of the above Francis Dobson 8th day]

Jennet Kempe decimo die
[Jennet Kempe (Kemp) 10th day]

Johes Scoles et Georgius Webster decimo quinto die
[John Scoles and George Webster 15th day]

Robfũs Mylner (vicesimo nono die)
[Robert Mylner (29th day [faded at bottom of column])]

Weddinges	Christeninges	Burials
Thomas Owen et Catherina Robinson decimo septimo die	Pettus filius Willmi Webster de Pothwell primo die. Alicia Dickinson nono die.	Antonius Robinson tertio die.
Tho: Moxon et Jean Stanfeild decimo quarto die	filia Johis Eyrde decimo die	Pettus Webster filius Thome Webster decimo quarto die
Johes Brooke vid et ... et Anna Corbett vicesimo sexto die	Anna filia Ric Wright decimo septimo die	

december

Weddinges	Christeninges	Burialls
Pettus Wilson et Alicia Smyth primo die.	Anna filia Johis Spencer primo die. Maria filia Johis Huley secundo die. Agnes filia Thome Swisse quarto die. Isabella filia Willmi fforman decimo quarto die. Maria filia Thome Heptenstall et Tho: filius Jacobi Dobson de Charlton ... 25 die. Pirus filius Robti	Francis Dobson filiol 7 die
Pettus Sherharde et Anna Townend 3ro die.		Agnes ux vxor Francisci Dobson octavo die
Tho: Brookthorpe et Jennett Baxter		Jennet Kempe decimo die.
Robtus Clarke et Margareta Fox		Johes Broles et Georgius Webster decimo quinto die
Georgius Benton et Joan Dixon decimo die		Robtus Mylne ... nono die

List of Selected Latin Given Names

LATIN NOMINATIVE (principal)	LATIN GENITIVE (son, dau, of)	LATIN ABLATIVE (son, dau, by)	ENGLISH
Adamus	Adami	Adamo	Adam
Adam	Ade	Ada	Adam
Ademarus	Ademari	Adamora	Aymer
Adhelina	Adhelinae	Adhelina	Adeline
Adomarus	Adomari	Adomaro	Aymer
Aegidius	Aegidii	Aegidio	Giles
Agelwinus	Agelwini	Agelwino	Aylwin
Agnes	Agnetis	Agnete	Agnes
Ailbertus	Ailberti	Ailberto	Ethelbert, Albert
Ailmaricus	Ailmarici	Ailmarico	Emery
Ailmerus	Ailmeri	Ailmero	Aylmer
Alanus	Alani	Alano	Alan
Alberedus	Alberedi	Alberedo	Alfred
Albaricus	Albarici	Albarico	Aubrey
Albinus	Albini	Albino	Aubyn
Albredus	Albredi	Albredo	Aubrey
Alexander	Alexandri	Alexandro	Alexander
Alianora	Alianorae	Alionora	Eleanor
Aloysius	Aloysii	Aloysio	Lewis
Aluredus	Aluredi	Aluredo	Alfred
Alricus	Alrici	Alrico	Elfric
Amabilla	Amabillae	Amabilla	Mabel
Ambrosius	Ambrosii	Ambrosio	Ambrose
Amia	Amiae	Amia	Amy
Amicia	Amiciae	Amicia	Amice
Amicius	Amicii	Amicio	Amyas
Anabilia	Anabiliae	Anabilia	Annabel
Andreas	Andreae	Andrea	Andrew
Andreus	Andrei	Andreo	Andrew
Anicia	Aniciae	Anicia	Annis
Anthonius	Anthonii	Anthonio	Anthony
Araldus	Araldi	Araldo	Harold
Arcturus	Arcturi	Arcturo	Arthur
Artorius	Artorii	Artorio	Arthur
Archibaldus	Archibaldi	Archibaldo	Archibald
Audoinus	Audoini	Audoino	Owen
Audomarus	Audomari	Audomaro	Omer
Augustinus	Augustini	Augustino	Austin
Avicia	Aviciae	Avicia	Avis
Bartholomaeus	Bartholomaei	Bartholomaeo	Bartholomew
Basilius	Basilii	Basilii	Basil
Baudwinus	Baudwini	Baudwino	Baldwin
Benedictus	Benedicti	Benedicto	Bennet
Bevicius	Bevicii	Bevicio	Bevis
Blasius	Blasii	Blasio	Blaise
Bogo	Bogonis	Bogone	Bew, Bevis, Boeges
Brianus	Briani	Briuno	Brian
Bricius	Bricii	Bricio	Brice
Brigitta	Brigittae	Brigitta	Bridget

LATIN NOMINATIVE (principal)	LATIN GENITIVE (son, dau, of)	LATIN ABLATIVE (son, dau, by)	ENGLISH
Caecilia	Caeciliae	Caecilia	Cecily
Caecilius	Caecilii	Caecilio	Cecil
Caius	Caii	Caio	Kay
Cananus	Canani	Canano	Kynan
Carolus	Caroli	Carolo	Charles
Cedde	Ceddenis	Ceddene	Chad
Christophorus	Christophori	Christopho	Christopher
Colandus	Colandi	Colando	Colin
Creatura, e (used in hasty baptisms to serve for either sex).			
Cudbertus	Cudberti	Cudberto	Cuthbert
Cuthbertus	Cuthberti	Cuthberto	Cuthbert
Desiderius	Desiderii	Desiderio	Didier
Danielus	Danieli	Danielo	Daniel
Davidus	Davidi	Davido	David
Dionysius	Dionysii	Dionysio	Dennis
Dermicius	Dermicii	Dermicio	Dermot
Draco	Draconis	Dracone	Drew
Drugan	Druganis	Drugane	Drue
Dunechanus	Dunechani	Dunechano	Duncan
Duvenaldus	Duvenaldi	Duvenaldo	Donald
Eadmundus	Eadmundi	Eadmundo	Edmund
Eadwardus	Eadwardi	Eadwardo	Edward
Ebulo	Ebulonis	Ebulono	Eble, Euball
Edenevettus	Edenevetti	Edenevetto	Edneved
Edmundus	Edmundi	Edmundo	Edmund
Edwardus	Edwardi	Edwardo	Edward
Egidius	Egidii	Egidio	Giles
Elfredus	Elfredi	Elfredo	Alfred
Elias	Eliae	Elia	Ellis, Elias
Elizeus	Elizii	Elizio	Ellis, Elias
Elias	Eliatis	Eliate	Ellis, Elias
Emelina	Emelinae	Emelina	Emily
Emericus	Emerici	Emerico	Emery
Erniscus	Ernisii	Ernisio	Ernest
Ethelreda	Ethelredae	Ethelreda	Audrey
Eudo	Eudonis	Eudone	Eudes
Eustachius	Eustachii	Eustachio	Eustace
Eva	Evae	Eva	Eve
Falcho	Falchonis	Falchone	Falk
Felicia	Feliciae	Felicia	Felise
Fides	Fidei	Fide	Faith
Francicus	Francici	Francico	Francis
Francus	Franci	Franco	Frank
Fridericus	Friderici	Friderico	Frederick
Fulcho	Fulchonis	Fulchone	Fulk
Fulqueyus	Fulqueyi	Fulqueyo	Fulk
Galfridus	Galfridi	Galfrido	Geoffrey
Galterus	Galteri	Galtero	Walter

LATIN NOMINATIVE (principal)	LATIN GENITIVE (son, dau, of)	LATIN ABLATIVE (son, dau, by)	ENGLISH
Galwanus	Galwani	Galwano	Gawain
Garinus	Garini	Garino	Warren
Gaufridus	Gaufridi	Gaufrido	Geoffrey
Gawtherus	Gawtheri	Gawthero	Walter
Georgius	Georgii	Georgio	George
Gerardus	Gerardi	Gerardo	Gerard
Germanus	Germani	Germano	Germain, Garmon
Geroldus	Geroldi	Geroldo	Gerald
Gervasius	Gervasii	Gervasio	Gervase
Gilebertus	Gileberti	Gileberto	Gilbert
Ginevra	Ginevrae	Ginevra	Guenever
Giselbertus	Giselberti	Giselberto	Gilbert
Godefridus	Godefridi	Godefrido	Godfrey
Godelacius	Godelacii	Godelocio	Guthlac
Goscelinus	Goscelini	Goscelino	Jocelyn
Gosfridus	Gosfridi	Gosfrido	Geoffrey
Grahamus	Grahami	Grahamo	Graham
Gregorius	Gregorii	Gregorio	Gregory
Griffinus	Griffini	Griffino	Griffith
Gualterus	Gualteri	Gualtero	Walter
Guarinus	Guarini	Guarino	Warren
Guido	Guidonis	Guidone	Guy
Guilfridus	Guilfridi	Guilfrido	Wilford
Guilielmus	Guilielmi	Guilielmo	William
Hamo	Hamonis	Hamone	Hamon
Haraldus	Haraldi	Haraldo	Harold
Hasculfus	Hasculfi	Hasculfo	Hascoil
Hawisia	Hawisiae	Hawisia	Hawise
Helewisa	Helewisae	Helewisa	Helewis
Helyas	Heliae	Helia	Ellis
Henricus	Henrici	Henrico	Henry
Hereweccus	Herewecci	Herewecco	Hervey
Hervieus	Herviei	Hervieo	Hervy
Hieremias	Hieremiae	Hieremia	Jeremiah
Hieremias	Hieremiatis	Hieremiate	Jeremiah
Hieronymus	Hieronymi	Hieronymo	Jerome
Hilarius	Hilarii	Hilario	Hilary
Honoria	Honoriae	Honoria	Honor
Hugo	Hugonis	Hugone	Hugh
Hugonis ⎱ Hugonus ⎰	Hugoni	Hugono	Hugh
Humfredus	Humfredi	Humfredo	Humphrey
Ingelramus	Ingelrami	Ingelramo	Ingram
Isolda	Isoldae	Isoldae	Isault, Isouda
Ingeramus	Ingerami	Ingeramo	Ingram
Ismahel	Ismahelis	Ismaheli	Ishmael
Ivo	Ivonis, Ivetis	Ivone, Ivete	Ives
Jacobus	Jacobi	Jacobo	Jacob, James
Jeruerdus	Jeruerdi	Jeruerdo	Jurwerth
Joceus	Jocei	Joceio	Joyce
Jodoca	Jodocae	Jodoca	Joyce

LATIN NOMINATIVE (principal)	LATIN GENITIVE (son, dau, of)	LATIN ABLATIVE (son, dau, by)	ENGLISH
Jodocus	Jodoci	Jodoco	Joyce
Johanna	Johannae	Johanna	Joan, Jane
Johannes	Johanni	Johanno	John
Jonathas	Jonathae	Jonatha	Jonathan
Josias	Josie, Josiatis	Josia, Josiate	Josiah
Judas	Judae, Judatis	Juda, Judate	Jude
Judocus	Judoci	Judoco	Josse
Justinus	Justini	Justino	Justin
Kananus	Kanani	Kanano	Kynan
Kanaucus	Kanauci	Kanauco	Cynog
Karadocus	Karadoci	Karadoco	Caradog
Kenewricus	Kenewrici	Kenewrico	Cynvrig
Kenulmus	Kenulmi	Kenulmo	Kenelm
Laetitia	Laetitiae	Laetitia	Lettice, Letitia
Lancilottus	Lancilotti	Lancilotto	Lancelot
Landebertus	Landeberti	Landeberto	Lambert
Laurentius	Laurenti	Laurentio	Lawrence
Leodgardus	Leodgardi	Leodgardo	Ledger
Leonellus	Leonelli	Leonello	Lionel
Leudocus	Leudoci	Leudoco	Llawddogor, Lleuddad
Levelinus	Levelini	Levelino	Llewelyn
Ligerius	Ligerii	Ligerio	Leger
Lionhardus	Lionhardi	Lionhardo	Leonard
Lorentius	Lorenti	Lorentio	Lawrence
Lucas, Lucasius	Lucae, Lucasii	Luka, Lucasio	Luke
Ludovicus	Ludovici	Ludovico	Lewis
Luolinus	Luolini	Luolino	Llewelyn
Mabilla, Mabilia	Mabillae, Mabiliae	Mabilla, Mabilia	Mabel
Machutus	Machuti	Machuto	Mawe
Madocus	Madoci	Madoco	Madog
Maidocus	Maidoci	Maidoco	Madog
Marcus	Marci	Marco	Mark
Margeria	Margeriae	Margeria	Margery
Marta	Martae	Marta	Martha
Mathaeus	Mathaei	Mathaeo	Matthew
Matildis	Matildis	Matildi	Matilda, Maud
Matilda	Matildae	Matilda	Matilda
Mauditus	Mauditi	Maudito	Mawe
Mauricius	Mauricii	Mauricio	Morris
Meilerious	Meilerii	Meilerio	Meilyr
Mercia	Merciae	Mercia	Mercy
Mereducius	Mereducii	Mereducio	Meredith
Merinus	Merinii	Merino	Mervyn
Meuricius	Meuricii	Meuricio	Maurice
Michaelis	Michaelis	Michaeli	Michael
Misericordia	Misericordiae	Misericordia	Mercy
Mordacus	Mordaci	Mordaco	Mordac
Moreducus	Moreduci	Moreduco	Meredith
Morganus	Morgani	Morgano	Morgan
Moyses	Moysis	Moysi	Moses
Mungo	Mungonis	Mungone	Mungo

LATIN NOMINATIVE (principal)	LATIN GENITIVE (son, dau, of)	LATIN ABLATIVE (son, dau, by)	ENGLISH
Natalis	Natalis	Natali	Noel
Nathan	Nathanis	Nathane	Nathan
Nicolaa	Nicolaae	Nicolaa	Nicola
Nicolaus	Nicolai	Nicolao	Nicholas
Nigellus	Nigelli	Nigello	Nigel
Normannus	Normanni	Normanno	Norman
Odo	Odinis	Odine	Eudes
Oenus	Oeni	Oeno	Owen
Olaus	Olai	Olao	Olaf
Oliverus	Oliveri	Olivero	Oliver
Omfreidus	Omfreidi	Omfreido	Humphrey
Owinus	Owini	Owino	Owen
Paganus	Pagani	Pagano	Pain
Pancratius	Pancratii	Pancratio	Pancras
Paternus	Paterni	Paterno	Padarn
Patricius	Patricii	Patricio	Patrick
Pero	Peronis	Perone	Piers
Petrus	Petri	Petro	Peter
Prudentia	Prudentiae	Prudentia	Prudence
Quaspatricius	Quaspatricii	Quaspatricio	Gospatrick
Radulfus	Radulfi	Radulfo	Ralph
Randolphus	Randolphi	Randolpho	Randolph, Randall
Reginaldus	Reginaldi	Reginaldo	Reginald, Reynold
Regulus	Reguli	Regulo	Rule
Reinerus	Reineri	Reineri	Rayner
Resus	Resi	Reso	Rhys
Richardus	Richardi	Richardo	Richard
Rogerus	Rogeri	Rogero	Roger
Robertus	Roberti	Roberto	Robert
Rohelendus	Rohelendi	Rohelendo	Roland
Rothericus	Rotherici	Rotherico	Roderick
Salomon	Salomonis	Salomoni	Solomon
Samuel	Samuelis	Samuele	Samuel
Sativolus	Sativoli	Sativolo	Sidwell
Savarus	Savari	Savaro	Saier
Saul	Saulis	Saule	Saul
Seisillas	Seisilli	Seisillo	Cecil
Sewallus	Sewalli	Sewallo	Sewell
Sibella	Sibellae	Sibella	Sybil
Sidneus	Sidnei	Sidneo	Sidney
Silvanus	Silvani	Silvano	Silas
Stephanus	Stephani	Stephano	Stephen
Suanas	Suani	Suano	Swein
Symon	Symonis	Symone	Simon
Tedbaldus	Tedbaldi	Tedbaldo	Theobald
Teleaucus	Teleauci	Teleauco	Teilo
Teodoricus	Teodorici	Teodorico	Thierri

LATIN NOMINATIVE (principal)	LATIN GENITIVE (son, dau, of)	LATIN ABLATIVE (son, dau, by)	ENGLISH
Terricus	Terrici	Terrico	Thierry, Terrence
Theobaldus	Theobaldi	Theobaldo	Theobald, Tybalt
Theodorus	Theodori	Theodoro	Theodore, Tudor
Thomas	Thomae	Thoma	Thomas
Timotheus	Timothei	Timotheo	Timothy
Tobias	Tobiae, Tobiatis	Tobia, Tobiate	Tobias
Tobius	Tobii	Tobio	Toby
Turstanus	Turstani	Turstano	Thurstan
Ulitius	Ulitii	Ulitio	Ulick
Umfridus	Umfridi	Umfrido	Humphrey
Vadinus	Vadini	Vadino	Valentine
Vedastus	Vedasti	Vedasto	Foster
Villefredus	Villefredi	Villefredo	Wilfrid
Vincentius	Vincentii	Vincento	Vincent
Vitalis	Vitalis	Vitali	Hagin
Vulstanus	Vulstani	Vulstano	Wulfstan
Waco	Waconis	Wacone	Wake
Wandregisilus	Wandregisili	Wandregisilo	Wandril
Warnerus	Warneri	Warnero	Warner
Wido	Widonis	Widone	Guy
Wilhelmus	Wilhelmi	Wilhelmo	William
Yuo	Yuonis	Yuone	Ives
Yvonus	Yvoni	Yvono	Ives

In early records the dates, amounts of money, and other figures are often written in Latin. The Roman symbols are written either in capitals (XIV, XXII, MDCCLII) or in lower-case letters (xiv, xxii, mdcclii). The following table is a useful reference:

ROMAN NUMERALS	CARDINALS	ORDINALS	
	Nominative	Nominative	Ablative
I	unus, -a, -um	1st primus, -a, -um	primo (*on the first*)
II	duo, duae, duo	2nd secundus (alter)	secundo
III	tres, tria	3rd tertius	tertio
IV, IIII	quattuor	4th quartus	quarto
V	quinque	5th quintus	quinto
VI	sex	6th sextus	sexto
VII	septem	7th septimus	septimo
VIII	octo	8th octavus	octavo
IX, VIIII	novem	9th nonus	nono
X	decem	10th decimus	decimo
XI	undecim	11th undecimus	undecimo
XII	duodecim	12th duodecimus	duodecimo
XIII	tredecim	13th tertius decimus	tertio decimo
XIV, XIIII	quattuordecim	14th quartus decimus	quarto decimo
XV	quindecim	15th quintus decimus	quinto decimo
XVI	sedecim	16th sextus decimus	sexto decimo
XVII	septemdecim	17th septimus decimus	septimo decimo
XVIII	duodeviginti	18th duodevicesimus	duodevicesimo
XIX, XVIIII	undeviginti	19th undevicesimus	undevicesimo
XX	viginti	20th vicesimus	vicesimo
XXI	viginti unus, unus et viginti[1]	21st vicesimus primus, unus et vicesimus	vicesimo primo
XXII	viginti duo, duo et viginti	22nd vicesimus secundus, alter et vicesimus	vicesimo secundo

---

[1] In English it was often the custom to say "one and twenty," as in "four and twenty blackbirds."

ROMAN NUMERALS	CARDINALS	ORDINALS	
	Nominative	Nominative	Ablative
XXIII	viginti tres	23rd vicesimus tertius	vicesimo tertio
XXIV, XXIIII	viginti quattuor	24th vicesimus quartus	vicesimo quarto
XXV	viginti quinque	25th vicesimus quintus	vicesimo quinto
XXVI	viginti sex	26th vicesimus sextus	vicesimo sexto
XXVII	viginti septem	27th vicesimus septimus	vicesimo septimo
XXVIIII	viginti octo, duodetriginta	28th vicesimus octavus, duodetricesimus	duodetricesimo
XXIX, XXVIIII	viginti novem, undetriginta	29th vicesimus nonus, undetricesimus	undetricesimo
XXX	triginta	30th tricesimus	tricesimo
XXXI	triginta unus, unus et triginta	31st tricesimus primus, unus et tricesimus	tricesimo primo
XL, XXXX	quadraginta	40th quadragesimus	
L	quinquaginta	50th quinquagesimus	
LX	sexaginta	60th sexagesimus	
LXX	septuaginta	70th septuagesimus	
LXXX, XXC	octoginta	80th octogesimus	
LXXXX, XC	nonaginta	90th nonagesimus	
C	(100) centum	100th centesimus	
CI	(101) centum (et) unus	101st centesimus (et) primus	
CL	(150) centum quinquaginta	150th centesimus quinquagesimus	
CC	(200) ducenti, -ae, -a	200th ducentesimus	
CCC	(300) trecenti	300th trecentesimus	
CD, CCCC	(400) quadringenti	400th quadringentesimus	
D, IↃ	(500) quingenti	500th quingentesimus	
DC, IↃC	(600) sescenti	600th sescentesimus	
DCC, IↃCC	(700) septingenti	700th septingentesimus	
DCCC	(800) octingenti	800th octingentesimus	
DCCCC, CM	(900) nongenti	900th nongentesimus	
M, CIↃ	(1000) mille	1000th millesimus	

Latin Terms and Their Meanings

Latin	*English*
a, ab, abs	from, away from, down from, out of, by
a sinistrus	at the left
ab hoc mense	from this month on
abavia	2nd great-grandmother
abavus, atavus	2nd great grandfather or ancestor
abhinc	from hence
abinde	thenceforward, thereafter
abortivus	prematurely born
ac	and
acicularius, acuarius	needle maker
ad	to, at, in, before, for, towards
ad festum	at the feast
adhuc	thus far, hitherto, as yet, still
adolescens	young man
adulter	adulterer
adultera	adultress
adulterium	adultery
advenae, advena, advenus	of a stranger or foreigner
adventus	advent, arrival, appearance at court
advocatus (adv.)	advocate or witness
aedilis	architect (public works officer)
aedituus	church guardian
aetas	age, period of time
aetate minoris	ycungest son by age, Jr.
aetatis (aet.)	of age
affinitas	relative in law
agnatus	blood relative in male line
agricola	farmer
alias, alia, aliud	otherwise, or, another
alienus	otherwise, alias (likewise), or
aliter	other, another
alius, alia, aliud	student (also inhabitant)
alumnus	tanner
alutarius	both (of this parish, etc.)
ambo	foreign, stranger
amicitia	relationship, friendship
amita	aunt, father's sister
amita, magna	grandfather's sister
ancilla	female servant, maid
anniversarium	anniversary
anno domini	in the year of the Lord
annus, anno, anni	year, in the year, of the year

Latin	*English*
annus bissextus (bissextilis)	leap year
annutatim, annuus etc.	annual
anonymus, anonyma	stillborn son or daughter
antea	formerly
antecessor	ancestor or predecessor
antedictus	aforesaid
anti, ante	before
antiquus	old, ancient, senior
antistes	director, bishop
anus	old woman
apothecarius	pharmacist
apud	in, near by, at, to, before
apud acta	by the acts of court
aquaria, aquae	water carrier, water
arbiter	witness, arbitrator
archiater	physician
archididascalus	headmaster
archidiaconus	archdeacon
archiepiscopus	archbishop
architectus	architect, builder
arcularius	carpenter
armentarius	herdsman
armiger	gentleman, squire, esquire, shield bearer, knight
aromatarius	druggist, perfume maker
ut asseritur	as it is asserted
atque	and
attornatus	attorney
aurifaber	goldsmith
auriga	driver
aurigifex	wagon maker
avi	ancestor or grandfathers
avia	grandmother
avunculus	uncle (mother's brother)
avunculus major	granduncle, grandmother's brother
avus	grandfather
bacallarius	bachelor
baccalaureus (Bacc.)	university degree B.A.
ballistrarius	gunmaker
baptisatus (baptista, bapt.)	baptized, christened
baro, baronis	freeman, baron
bedellus	beadle
beneficium	feudal estate, or slave, or ecclesiastical benefice
bercarius	shepherd, sheepfold

Latin	English
bibliopegus	bookbinder
biennium	2 year period
bonus, bona	good, goods
bordarius	bordar, tenant
brasiator	brewer
burgensis, burgarus	burgess in a borough
bursarius	treasurer
caelebs (coelebs)	single or widowed (of either sex)
calciator	shoemaker
camerarius	valet, groom
campanator	bell ringer
canon	canon
capella	chapel
capellanus	chaplain
capitaneus	captain
capitis, caput	head
capt et jurat	taken and sworn
captivus	prisoner
carbonarius	collier or coal miner
carecarius	carter, ploughman
carnifex	hangman, executioner
carpentarius	carpenter, cartwright
carta	deed or chart, map
caupo, cauponinis	innkeeper
caupona	inn
chartarius	paper miller
chirotherarus	glover
chirurgus	surgeon
cingarus	Gypsy, Egyptian
cippus	gravestone
circa (cir.)	about, around
circumforancus	tinker
civic (civ.), civis	citizen
claustrarius, clostrarius	locksmith
claviger, clavigeri	servant, key carrier, key bearer to St. Peter
clericus (cler.)	clergyman
cocus, coquus, coctor	cook
coelebs (coel)	unmarried, single
coemeterio	churchyard
coemeterium	cemetery
cognatio, cognationis	known, compensation for death of kinsmen
cognatus	blood relationship
cognomen, cognomunis	name, nickname
collega	guild, merchant, partner, college teacher, college or canons or cardinals

Latin	*English*
colonus	settler, farmer, peasant
colorator	dyer
comes, comitis	count, earl
comitatus (co., com., compt.)	county
comitissa	countess
commater	god-mother, sponsor
commuratis	fornication
compater	god-father, sponsor
concionator	preacher
conditio, conditionis	profession, gift, grant, a state or condition
conditus	honorable
conjug:	married (often indicates parents of child are married)
conjugata	married woman
conjuges	married couple
conjuncti fuere	they were married
conjunx	husband, wife
consanguinitas	blood relationship
ccnsobrinus, consobrina	cousin
constabularius	constable, warden
consul (regens)	count, earl, mayor, president of guild
contra	against, opposite
contractio	marriage, marriage contract
cooperta	married (of a woman)
copulatio	marriage ceremony
copulatus, copulato (cop.)	the married man or woman
coquus, cocus, coctor	cook
coram	before, in the presence of
corarius	currier
coriarius, courearius	tanner
corpus, corporis	(dead) body
cotarius	cottager
crysomme	a child whose mother is unchurched after birth of child
cuius suspectores	whose god-parents
cuius	whose, which, what
cuiusdam	of a certain
cultellarius	cutler
culter, or cultor	farmer or agricultural laborer
cum	with or when
cuprifaber	coppersmith
curator	guardian
curia	court, office
currifex	cartwright

Latin	*English*
cursor	messenger
custos	custodian, guardian
d.s.p., d. sine prole	died without issue
d.v.m., d. vita matris	died while mother was living
d.v.p., d. vita patris	died while father was living
datum (d.)	given
de	of, concerning, from
de prope	near
decanatus	deanery
decanus	deacon
decennarius	tithing-man
decessus	lease, demise, death
dedit	he or she has given
deforcians	deforcer
defunctus, defuncta	deceased, dead
denarius	coin, penny, money
denatus, denata	dead person
denunciatio	publication of banns
Deus	God
dexter	right (as opposed to left)
dictus	named, the said
didymi	twins
dies	day
die	on the day
die Lune	on the day of the moon — Monday
die Marti	on Tuesday
die Mecurio, die Wodenis	on Wednesday
die Jove	on Thursday
die Veneri	on Friday
die Saturno	on Saturday
die Sole	on Sunday
dispensator	steward
dixit	said
doageria	dowager
doleator	cooper
domesticus	domestic servant, inmate
domicellus	junker
domina	lady, mistress
dominica, dies dominicus	Sunday, day of the Lord
dominus	Sir, master, Lord
domuncularius	inmate, resident
domus	house
donatio	deed or gift
dux	duke or leader
dynastes	noblemen

Latin	*English*
e, ex	from, out of
ead, eodem	same (day), on the same
ecclesia (eccl.)	church
ego	I
eius, ejus	of this, him, his, her, it
eiusdem diei	of the same day
emeritorious	worthy
emeritus	out of service, pensioned off
ensifex	armourer, bearer of arms
epicedium	tribute, memorial
episcopus	bishop
eques	cavalry soldier
ergo	consequently, therefore
est	it is
et	and
et cetera (etc.)	and other things, and so forth
etiam	also, even
exitus	offspring, result, end
extra	outside
extraneus	stranger, foreign
faber	smith
faber ferrarius	blacksmith
faber cupri	coppersmith
faber lignarius	carpenter, charcoal burner
faber aerarius	tinker
familiaris	relative, slave, friend, follower
famula	female servant
famulus	male servant
femina	woman
feria (fer.)	day of fair or holiday
festum, festivitas	feast, wedding
fidejussor	god-parent
fidelis	a loyal, faithful, lasting
figulus	potter
filia	daughter
filia populae	illegitimate daughter
filiaster	stepson, son-in-law
filie or filiae	daughters
filiola	god-daughter
filiolus	god-son
filius	son
filius populi	illegitimate son
firmarius	farmer, renter
focus	hearth
fodiator, fossor, fossator	ditch digger, grave digger, miner

Latin	*English*
folium	sheet, thin foil of metal, one side of double seal
forestarius	forester
fossor, fossotor, fodiator	ditch digger, grave digger, miner
frater	brother
frater germanus	own or full brother
fuerant	had been
fuit	he, she, it was
funarius	rope maker
garcio	boy, servant, groom
gardianus	church warden
gemellae	female twins
gemelli, gemini	twins
gener	son-in-law or grandson-in-law
generosa	lady
generosus	gentleman, of noble birth, or servant of good birth
genitor, genitoris	begotten, parent
genitores	parents
gens	clan or families of common descent, people, followers, nation, stock
genus	sex, descent, offspring
germanus, germana	full brother, full sister
gnota, gnotus	illegitimate
gravida	pregnant
hac, haec	this
haereticus	heretic
hebdomada	week
heres, heredes, hereditaria	heir, heirs, heiress
hic	this
homicidium	murder
homo	man
honestus	honorable
hora	hour
hortulanus, horticola	gardener
hospes	host, stranger, tenant
hue usque	always of this place
huius, hujus	of this (man, woman, thing, place)
humatus, humata	buried
hypodidasculus	schoolmaster, usher
ib, ibid, ibidem	in the same place, moreover
ictus	a stroke, blow scholar of law, beat
id est (i.e.)	that is

Latin	*English*
ignata quaedam	a certain unknown woman
ignoti	illegitimate
ignoti parentis	of unknown parents
ignotus	unknown
ille de	he was from
ille fuit	he was
illegitimus, illegitima	illegitimate, unlawful
illustris	illustrious
immobilia	real estate, immovable goods
impedimentum consenguinitatis	hindrance of a relative
impotens ignotus	feeble minded
impraegnata	pregnant before marriage
imprimis, primus	the first
in	in, on
in capite	in chief, chiefly
in patria	in home town, native land
incerti cognominis	of uncertain surname
incipientes	beginning
incola, inquilinus	inhabitant
ineunte	in the beginning, in entering
infans	infant
infans ignotus	unknown infant
infra	within, below, lower
ingenuus	freeman, yeoman, freeborn
inhumatus	unburied
initiatus	baptized
inominata, inominatus	unnamed daughter, unnamed son
inguilinus, incola	inhabitant
institor	broker, factor, peddler, grocer
inter	between, among
inupta	not married
ipse	himself herself
ipse dixit	as he asserted
istius	of this
item, it., itm	also, likewise
jam	already, now
janitor	janitor
judex	judge
judica	judgments
junior (jun.)	junior
juramentus exhibitum fuit	certificate was produced or sworn to (buried in wool)
jurator	juror
juravit	has sworn
juris utriusque doctor (J.U.D.)	doctor of laws

Latin	English
jurisconsultus	lawyer, jurist
jus civile (civitatis) or civilis	the common law
jus civitatis adepti sunt	right of the state having been obtained, taken out citizenship papers
juvenis (juv.)	young man, bachelor
laborator	laborer
lanatus	clothed in wool (espec. for "buried in wool")
lanio, laniator	falconry, butcher
lapicida, lapidarius	stone mason, stone cutter
laterarius	tile maker, bricklayer
levans	god-parent
liber	book, free
liber baro	Lord
liber rusticus	free peasant
liberalis	free, free-born
liberi, liberorum	freeman, children
librarius, librarian	book dealer
lictor	town official
ligatus	confederate, conspirator, husband
lignarius	joiner, cabinetmaker
linifex, lintearius	linen weaver
locus, locorum, loco	place, of places, in the place
lorarius	saddler
lota, lotus	to bathe, to wash (baptise)
ludi magister, ludi moderator	schoolmaster
magister	master
magna, magnus	great, senior, the elder
majores	ancestors, elder
mandatum	order
mansus	piece of land or dwelling house
manu propria (m.p. mria)	signed personally, by one's own hand
maritatio	marriage
mariti	married couple
maritus conjunx	husband
martia	wife
mater	mother
mater meretrix	illegitimate mother
matertera	mother's sister, aunt
matrimonium	matrimony
matrina, materna	god-mother
matura	mature
maximus natu	first born
media	the middle

Latin	*English*
medicus	physician
mendicus	begger
mensa	table
mens, mensis	month, of the month
mente captus	insane, deceased in mind
mercator	merchant, trader
meretrix	harlot
miles, miletis	soldier, knight
miles gregarius	private soldier
militis proles	soldier's child
minimus a natu	youngest born
ministeriales	vassals, commissionaires
minoris	junior
minuta	minutes
modius	a measure — a peck
mola, molendinum, molina	mill
molendinarius, molitor	miller
monachus	monk
monialis	nun
monumentum	monument
more novo (m.n.)	in the new manner, new reckoning style (of dates)
more vetere (m.v.)	in the old way, old reckoning style (of dates)
moritur	having died
mors, mortis	death
mortuus, mortua	deceased, dead, died
mulier	woman
murarius, murator	mason
natalis	birth
natio or natione	nationality, nation or birth
nativitas	birth
nativus	born, native
natu minoris	youngest son, Jr.
natu maioris	oldest son, Sr.
natus, nata	born (often used to indicate maiden surname)
nauta	sailor
navigor	sailor, navigator
necnon	and also
necnon	pauper
nee	French word indicating maiden surname
negotiator (extraneus)	trader, peddler, outside trader, merchants, etc.
neophytus	newly baptized
nepos, nepus	grandchild, nephew, descendant
neptis	granddaughter, niece, descendant

Latin	*English*
nihil	blank, nothing
nobilis	noble
nomen, nomine, nominis	name, by name, title
non-legitt., -legitimus, -legitima	illegitimate
nothus, nothis, nota	bastard, illegitimate
novercus, noverca	step-parent
nunc	now, at present
nunquam	never
nuntius	messenger
nuper	lately, formerly, recently (of)
nupt fuerant	were married
nuptiae	wedding
nurus	daughter-in-law
obiit (ob.)	he died
obiit eodem anno	died the same year
obiit repentina morte	died without sacrament (suddenly)
obitt sine prole	died without issue
obsequia	divine services, funeral
obstetrix	midwife
oeconomicus	economist, farmer
olim	formerly, hereafter, former (old or maiden name)
operarius	workman, laborer, tradesman, craftsman
opifex	laborer or artisan
oppidum	town, city
orbus, orba, orphanus	orphan
origo	origin
oriundus ex	arising or born from, tracing from
ovilius, oviliasus	shepherd
pacatio	payment
pactum	contract, treaty, pact, lease
pagare, paco	pay
pagina (p. pag.)	page of a book or leaf of paper
pagus	village
pannifex	cloth worker
papa	pope
parcarius robrarius	park keeper
parentes (p. par.)	parents, recent ancestors
paroch, parochia	parish
parochus	minister
parsona	minister
parvux, parva	small or little
pascaurrus	minister
passim	frequently

Latin	English
pastor	shepherd
pater	father
pater familias	householder
pater supputatus	supposed father
patre supputato	with or by the supposed father
patres	forefathers
in patria	in home town, native land
patrini, patrinis	god-parents or sponsors
patrino	god-father
patruelis	cousin on father's side
patruus	uncle
pauper	poor
pedalis	foot soldier
pellifex, pellio	furrier
penult	the last but one
per	through, by
percepta	received or collected, income
peregrinus	foreigner, traveler, wanderer
pergamenum	parchment
peritus	skilled
pictor	painter
pileator, pilio	hatter
piscator	fisherman
pistor	baker
pius	pious
placea	residence
placitum	resolution, a plea, pleasing
platea	alley, street
plebanus	minister, rural dean
plebs	common people
poeta	poet
pomerium, pomarium	orchard
pontificius	catholic, papal
popula, populi	common people
porcarius	swineherd
portio materna	maternal share or part of benefice
possessor	possessor
post	after
posteri	descendants
posteritas	descendency
posthumus, posthuma	born after father's death
postremo	last
postridie	the day after
praefectus orbis, praeter	mayor, official, overseer, baliff, steward
praematurus concubitus (pream. conc.)	illegal cohabitation

Latin	*English*
praesentibus	in presence of
praetorium	courthouse, council chamber
preco	appraiser, watchman, crier, preacher
predictus	aforesaid
prefatus	aforesaid
prefectus	reeve
prelatus	official, reeve
prepositus	reeve
pridie	the day before
primogenitor	first born
priores	ancestors
privignus	stepson from former marriage
pro tempore, tunc temporis	before or in the time, of that time
proavia	great-grandmother
proavus	great-grandfather
procreatus	begotten
procurator	monastic official, lawyer, proctor of university or consistorial courts
proles	offspring, descendant
proles spuria	illegitimate descendant
promotio	preferment, promotion
promulgatio	proclamation, marriage announcement
pronepos	great-grandson
prope	near
propinquarius	kinsman
propinquior	nearest relation
proprius	one's own, special, proper, personal
propter aetatem	on account of age
provincia	province, country
proximus	next
publicus	public
puella	maiden or girl
puer	boy
puera	girl
puerpera	women in childbirth
puerperium	childbirth, confinement, delivery, newborn infant
pupillus	motherless
puta	reputed, supposed, thought
quaestor	treasurer, paymaster
que	and
qui, quae, quod	who, which, what
quidam	a certain
quoad	how long, with respect to, how far, as far as
quod vide (q.v.)	see reference

Latin	*English*
quodam, quidam	of a certain (person)
quondam	the late, once upon a time, formerly
quoque	also
quorum	whose
regimine pedestre	infantry regiment
regina	queen
regius	royal
relicta (rel.)	widow
relictus	widower
reminiscere	to recall, to remember
renatus, renata	to be born again, baptized
requiescat in pace (r.i.p.)	rest in peace
restio, restarius	rope maker
reverendus	reverend
rex	king
roborarius custos	forester
rusticus	peasant
s.p. (d.s.p.)	died without issue
sacellanus	chaplain
sacerdos	priest
salarium	pay, salary
sanctus	holy
saponarius	soap maker
sartor	taylor
scannum	bank
scolaris	scholar
scorta	whore, harlot
scortun, scorta	skin, hide
scriba, scriptor	writer, secretary
scriba librarius	clerk
sculptor	sculptor
sedes	seat
seductor	seducer, debaucher
sellator	saddler
senex	old
senior (sen.)	the elder one
senoris	of the old
sepultus, sepulta	buried
sequens, sequenti	following, of the following
serarius	locksmith
serviens	servant of high rank
servus	servant, serf
sesquiannum	period of 1½ years
sexus	sex

Latin	*English*
sic	thus (doubtful name or date)
sigillum	seal
silvarius	forester
sine	without
a sinistrus	at the left
situs, sita	situated, located
sive, seu	or, if
smigarius	soap maker
sobrinus, sobrina	cousin on mother's side
socer	father-in-law
socius	associate, ally
socrinus	brother-in-law
socrus	mother-in-law or father-in-law
solemanicatio	solemnize, wedding ceremony
solidus	a shilling, the whole sum, solid
soror	sister
sororius	brother-in-law
sponsalia	dowry, marriage bands
sponsus, sponsa	husband, wife
sponsores sponsoribus	sponsors, by the sponsors
spuria, spurius, spuris (sp.)	illegitimate daughter or son
stemma, stemma gentile	pedigree
stirps	source, origin, offspring
strata	street
studiosus	student
stuprata	pregnant out of wedlock
sua	her own
sub	under
sub tutela	under guardianship
subditus	subject of a priest's or minister's congregation
suburbium	suburb
supra	above, higher, over
suscepit (susc.)	to receive, accept, out of baptism
susceptor, susceptrix	guardian, sponsor (at baptism), foster mother
sutor	shoemaker, cobbler
suus	his own
tabellarius	keeper of records
taberna	inn
templo, templum	in the church, church
pro tempore, tunc temporis	before or in the time, of that time
tempore belli	during war time
tempus	time

Latin	*English*
terrenus	tenant
territio-verbalis	cross examination
testamentum	will, probate
testimonium	testimony
testis	witness
textor	weaver
tinctor	dyer
tofta	toft, house-place
tomus	volume
tonsor	barber
tornator	turner
trigemini	triplets
trinitas	trinity
tritor	thrasher
tumulatus	buried
tunc temporis, pro tempore	before or in the time, of that time
tutor	guardian
ultimus, utimo (ulti'o, ult.)	last, on the last
um	the late
unicus	unique, only, sole
urbs	city
ut assitur, asseritur	as it is asserted
ut dicitur	as is said
uterque	both
ut ferter	as is reported
uxor, uxoris (ux.)	wife
uxor duxit	led his wife (in marriage)
uxoratus	married man, married
vagus	tramp, vagrant
variola	smallpox
vedovus	widower
vel	or
velle	will, testament
venator	hunter
venerabilis	honorable, adorable
vero	truly, indeed
vespilio	sexton or corpse bearer
vetula quaedam	a certain old woman
vetura, vetus	old
viator	traveler, tramp
vice	interchange, instead of, time, change
vicecomes	sheriff, reeve
viciatus	bastard

Latin	*English*
vicinus	neighbor, farmer
vicor	insane
vicus	village
vide	see
vide infra	see below
vide supra	see above
vidimus	we have seen
vivens	living
vidua, relicta	widow
viduus, relictus	widower
vietor	bind, to weaver, cooper
villanus	villein
villicus	a bailiff, overseer, inhabitant of village or farm
vir	man, husband
virgo	maiden, virgin
vistelator	fiddler, minstrel
vitriarius	glazier
vitricus (vitr.)	stepfather
vulgo	common, accessible to all, commonly known as
vulgus	the people, the public
vz	wife
w.	wife or widow
warda	guardianship
X	Christ
xped	christened
zonarius	girdle maker

A Selection of Saints' Days and Festivals Used in Dating

The influence of the medieval church in creating and observing saints' days and commemorating dates associated with the life of Christ led to the recording of events by reference to the feast day or saint's day rather than by the direct system of dating by day, month and year. For example, a parish register may say that John Smith was baptized on All Souls' Day 1641. Using the list that follows it can be readily determined that this boy was baptized 2 November 1641.

At the end of this list is a guide for finding the date of movable feast days and a calendar of feast days.

Advent Sunday	Sunday nearest to Feast of St. Andrew
All Hallows or All Saints Day	1 Nov
All Souls' Day	2 Nov
Andrew, Andreas, Andreae, apostle, Feast of	30 Nov
Anna, Anne, mother of Blessed Virgin Mary	26 July
Annunciatio of the Blessed Virgin Mary — Annunciatio dominica — Lady Day.	25 March
Ascension Day or Holy Thursday, Ascensio, Ascensa, domini (in celum)	Thursday following Rogation Sunday, 40 days after Easter
Ash Wednesday	1st day of Lent
Assumptio domini, Christi	Old name for Ascension Day
Black Monday	Easter Monday
Candlemas Day, Candelaria, Candelatio	2 Feb
Cantate	4th Sunday after Easter
Capitiluvium	Palm Sunday
Caput jejunii,	Ash Wednesday
Caramentranum, Caremprenium	Shrove Tuesday
Caresme	Lent (40 days of fasting)
Carnibrevium	Shrove Tuesday
Carniprivium novum	Quinquagesima Sunday
Carniprivium sacerdotum	Septuagesima Sunday
Carniprivium vetus	Quadragesima Sunday
Carnivora	Shrove Tuesday
Christmas Day	25 December
Circumdederunt	Septuagesima Sunday
Clausum Pentecostes	Trinity Sunday
Commovisti terram et conturbasti eam	Sexagesima Sunday
Corpus Christi or Body of Christ	Thurs. after Trinity Sunday
Crucis, Adoratio (or dies sancte crucis adorate, dies crucis adorande, veneris dis adoratus)	Good Friday
David of Wales, bishop and confessor.	1 March

Dies:

Adoratus	Good Friday
animarum (All Souls Day)	2 Nov
burarum	1st Sun. in Lent
cinerum	Ash Wednesday
crucis adorande, adorate	Good Friday
dominica, dominicus (Day of Our Lord)	Sunday or Easter Day
felicissimus	Easter Day
florum atque ramorum	Palm Sunday
jovis	Thursday
lune	Monday
magnus	Easter Day
mandati	Maundy Thursday
martis	Tuesday
mercurii, mercurinus, mercoris	Wednesday
osanne palmarum ramorum	Palm Sunday, 6th Sunday in Lent
sabbati	Saturday
sancte crucis adorate	Good Friday
veneris	Friday
veneris dies adoratus	Good Friday
Dimanche repus *or* reprus	Passion Sunday
Domine, ne longe	Palm Sunday
Dominica ad carnes levandas *or* tollendas	Quinquagesima Sunday
Dominica ante brandones	Quinquagesima Sunday
Dominica benedicta	Trinity Sunday
Dominica duplex	Trinity Sunday
Dominica indulgentie, indulgentiae	Palm Sunday
Dominica ramis palmarum	Palm Sunday
Dominica mediana	Passion Sunday
Dominica olivarum	Palm Sunday
Dominica osanna	Palm Sunday
Dominica in passione domini	Passion Sunday
Dominica Quadraginta	Quinquagesima Sunday
Dominica Rogationum	5th Sunday after Easter
Dominica sancta *or* Sancta in Pascha	Easter Sunday
Dominica sanctae trinitatis	Trinity Sunday
Easter (*see* Pascha)	
Edmund, Edmundus, King and Martyr	20 Nov
Epiphania domini, twelfth day	6 Jan
Epiphany, twelfth day	6 Jan
Esto mihi	Quinquargesima Sunday
Exaud	6th Sunday after Easter
Exsurge domine	Sexagesima Sunday
Fastmas, Fastren's Eve	Shrove Tuesday

Festum:

azymorum	Easter Day
Christi	Christmas
Eucharistie	Thursday before Easter
olivarum	Palm Sunday
omnium sanctorum (All Saints Day)	1 Nov
palmarum	Palm Sunday

Good Friday	Friday next before Easter
Hallowmas, Hallows, Hallontide (All Saints Day)	1 Nov
Hogmanay	31 Dec
Holy Friday (Good Friday)	Friday next before Easter
Holy Thursday	Ascension Day; Maundy Thursday

In palmis	Palm Sunday
Invocavit (Quadregesima)	6th Sunday before Easter
Isti sunt dies	Passion Sunday

Jacobi, Jacobus, James the Greater (Apostle and Martyr)	25 July
Jacobus, James the Less and Philip (Philippus et Jacobus)	1 May
Johannes, Johannis, John Apostle and evangelist	8 May & 27 Dec
Johannes, Johannis, John the Baptist:	
conception	24 Sept
nativity	24 June
beheading	29 Aug
Jour de pain perdu	Shrove Tuesday
Jour des Morts	All Souls' Day
Jour des Roys	The Epiphany
Jour du Saint Sacrament	Corpus Christi Day
Jubiliati	3rd Sunday after Easter
Judica me, Judica	Passion Sunday, 5th Sunday in Lent, 2nd before Easter

Lady Day	25 March
Lady, Our (See Mariae, Blessed Virgin)	
Lammas Day	1 Aug
Lataere	4th Sunday in Lent, 3rd before Easter

Lent (see Quadragesima)	
Lucas, Luke, evangelist	18 Oct

Marcus, Mark, evangelist	25 April
Maria, Mariae, Mary, Blessed Virgin:	
annunciation (Lady Day)	25 March

ascension or assumption	15 Aug
octave of assumption	22 Aug
conception	8 Dec
natale, nativitas, nativity	8 Sept. formerly 1 Jan.
octave of nativity	15 Sept
oblation	21 Nov
purification (Candlemas)	2 Feb
Matthaeus, Mattheus, Matthew, apostle and evangelist	21 Sept
Michael, Michaelis, archangel (Michael & All Angels) Michaelmas.	29 Sept
Midsummer Day	24 June
Midwinter Day	25 Dec
Misericordia	2nd Sunday after Easter
Nouvel Caresme	Quinquagesima Sunday
Oculi	3rd Sunday in Lent, 4th before Easter
Osanna	Palm Sunday
Palm Sunday, palmae *or* palmarum dies, in palmis	6th Sunday in Lent, 6th Sunday after Shrove Tues.
Pancake Tuesday	Shrove Tuesday
Paque charneux	Easter Day
Paque communiant, escommunichant, *or* communiaux	Easter Sunday
Paque de Noel	Christmas Day
Pascha	Easter Day, i.e., Sunday after full moon on or next after 21 March.[1]
Pascha competentium	
Pascha floridum, florum.	Palm Sunday
Pascha patitum	
Pascha rosarum	Pentecost
Passion Sunday	5th Sunday in Lent
Paul,, Pauli, Paulus, apostle of gentiles:	
commemoration	30 June
conversion	25 Jan
Pentecost (Whit-Sunday)	7th Sunday & 50th day after Easter Day
Peter, Petri, Petrus, ad vincula (in chains) at Rome	1 Aug
Philippus et Jacobus: Philip and James the Less, apostles	1 May

---

[1]Easter is a "movable feast," falling anywhere from March 22 through April 25 — a range of 35 days. Dependent on this variable Easter are 17 weeks of the ecclesiastical calendar. These "movable days" are listed in this selection of Saints' Days and Festivals.

Purification of Blessed Virgin Mary (Candlemas)	2 Feb
Quadragesima, Quadringesima (invocavit)	Lent, the 40 days preceding Easter
Quadragesima Sunday	1st Sunday in Lent, 6th Sunday before Easter
Quadraginta	Quinquagesima Sunday
Quasimodo	1st Sunday after Easter
Quinquagesima	Quinquagesima Sunday; also the 50 days from Easter to Pentecost, or the day of Pentecost.
Quinquagesima Sunday (Shrove Sunday)	Sunday before Ash Wednesday, 7th Sunday before Easter
Ramispalma	Palm Sunday
Reminissnere	2nd Sunday in Lent, 5th before Easter
Rogation Sunday	5th Sunday after Easter
(le) Roi des Dimanches	Trinity Sunday
Sancte in Pasche	Easter Sunday
Satirious	Easter Sunday
Septuagesima Sunday	9th Sunday before Easter
Sexagesima Sunday	8th Sunday before Easter
Shrove Tuesday	Tues. before Ash Wednesday
Solemnitas solemnitatum	Easter Day
Soulemas *or* Sowlemas Day (All Souls' Day)	2 Nov
Stephanus, Stephani, Stephen, protomartyr, feast of	26 Dec
Thomae, Thomas, apostle	21 Dec
Transfiguratio domini (Transfiguration of our Lord)	6 Aug
Trinitas estivalis	Trinity Sunday, 8th Sunday after Easter
Trinity Sunday	Sunday after Pentecost, 8th Sunday after Easter
Tryphayne	Epiphany (6 Jan)
Valentine	14 Feb
Vendredi, saint	Good Friday
Verid-sore (for) Vendredi-adore	Good Friday
Visitation of the Blessed Virgin Mary	2 July
Whit Sunday (Pentecost)	7th Sunday after Easter

GUIDE FOR FINDING THE DATE OF MOVABLE FEAST DAYS

J = Julian Calendar
G = Gregorian Calendar

Year	No.	Year	No.	Year	J	G	Year	J	G	Year	J	G	Year	J	G	Year	J	G	Year	J	G	Year	J	G	Year	No.	Year	No.	Year	No.
1528*	22	1555*	24	1582	25	25	1609	26	29	1636*	27	2	1663	29	4	1690	30	5	1717	31	7	1744#	4	15	1771	10	1798	18	1825	13
1529	7	1556*	15	1583	10	20	1610	18	21	1637	19	22	1664*	20	23	1691	22	25	1718	23	27	1745	24	28	1772*	29	1799	3	1826	5
1530	27	1557	28	1584*	29	11	1611	8	18	1638	4	14	1665	5	15	1692*	6	16	1719	8	19	1746	9	20	1773	21	1800	23	1827	25
1531	19	1558	20	1585	21	31	1612*	22	32	1639	24	34	1666	25	35	1693	26	1	1720*	27	23	1747	29	12	1774	13	1801	15	1828*	16
1532*	10	1559	5	1586	13	16	1613	14	17	1640*	15	18	1667	17	20	1694	18	21	1721	19	23	1748*	20	24	1775	26	1802	28	1829	29
1533	23	1560*	24	1587	26	8	1614	34	9	1641	35	10	1668*	1	11	1695	3	13	1722	4	15	1749	5	16	1776*	17	1803	20	1830	21
1534	15	1561	16	1588*	17	27	1615	19	29	1642	20	30	1669	21	31	1696*	22	32	1723	24	7	1750	25	8	1777	9	1804*	11	1831	13
1535	7	1562	8	1589	9	12	1616*	10	13	1643	12	15	1670	13	16	1697	14	17	1724*	15	26	1751	17	21	1778	29	1805	24	1832*	32
1536*	26	1563	21	1590	29	32	1617	30	5	1644*	31	6	1671	33	8	1698	34	8	1725	7	11	1752*	8	32	1779	14	1806	16	1833	17
1537	11	1564*	12	1591	14	24	1618	15	25	1645	16	26	1672*	17	27	1699	19	29	1726	20	31	1753	21	31	1780*	5	1807	8	1834	9
1538	31	1565	32	1592*	5	8	1619	7	10	1646	8	11	1673	9	12	1700#	11	21	1727	12	23	1754	13	24	1781	25	1808*	27	1835	29
1539	16	1566	24	1593	25	28	1620*	26	29	1647	28	31	1674	29	4	1701	30	6	1728*	31	7	1755	33	9	1782	10	1809	12	1836*	13
1540*	7	1567	9	1594	10	20	1621	11	21	1648*	12	22	1675	14	24	1702	15	26	1729	16	27	1756*	24	28	1783	30	1810	32	1837	5
1541	27	1568*	28	1595	30	5	1622	31	6	1649	4	14	1676*	5	15	1703	7	18	1730	8	19	1757	9	20	1784*	21	1811	24	1838	25
1542	19	1569	20	1596*	21	24	1623	23	26	1650	24	27	1677	25	28	1704*	26	2	1731	28	4	1758	29	5	1785	6	1812*	8	1839	10
1543	4	1570	5	1597	6	16	1624*	7	17	1651	9	19	1678	10	20	1705	18	22	1732*	19	23	1759	21	25	1786	26	1813	28	1840*	29
1544*	23	1571	25	1598	26	1	1625	27	9	1652*	28	10	1679	30	12	1706	3	14	1733	4	15	1760*	5	16	1787	18	1814	20	1841	21
1545	15	1572*	16	1599	18	21	1626	19	22	1653	20	28	1680*	21	31	1707	23	34	1734	24	35	1761	25	1	1788*	2	1815	5	1842	6
1546	35	1573	1	1600*	10	20	1627	4	14	1654	5	15	1681	13	16	1708*	14	18	1735	16	20	1762	17	21	1789	22	1816*	24	1843	26
1547	20	1574	21	1601	22	32	1628*	23	33	1655	25	7	1682	26	8	1709	34	10	1736*	35	11	1763	2	13	1790	14	1817	16	1844*	17
1548*	11	1575	13	1602	14	17	1629	15	25	1656*	16	26	1683	18	28	1710	19	30	1737	20	31	1764*	21	32	1791	34	1818	1	1845	2
1549	31	1576*	32	1603	34	9	1630	7	10	1657	8	11	1684*	9	12	1711	11	12	1738	12	16	1765	13	17	1792*	18	1819	21	1846	22
1550	16	1577	17	1604*	18	28	1631	20	30	1658	21	31	1685	29	32	1712*	30	6	1739	32	8	1766	33	9	1793	10	1820*	12	1847	14
1551	8	1578	9	1605	9	20	1632*	11	21	1659	13	23	1686	14	24	1713	15	26	1740*	16	27	1767	18	29	1794	30	1821	32	1848*	33
1552*	27	1579	29	1606	30	5	1633	31	6	1660*	32	6	1687	6	9	1714	7	11	1741	8	12	1768*	9	13	1795	15	1822	17	1849	18
1553	12	1580*	18	1607	15	25	1634	16	26	1661	24	27	1688*	25	28	1715	27	31	1742	28	4	1769	29	5	1796*	6	1823	9	1850	10
1554	4	1581	5	1608*	6	16	1635	8	18	1662	9	19	1689	9	19	1716*	13	20	1743	13	24	1770	14	25	1797	26	1824*	28	1851	30

NOTE: All years followed by an "*" are leap years.

#—The year 1700 was a leap year only in the localities still using the Julian Calendar. The year 1744 was a leap year on both the Julian and Gregorian Calendars, however Easter was celebrated a week apart in Germany and Denmark, thus the key for 1744 in Denmark and Norway under the Gregorian Calendar would be "8" instead of "15" as shown in the table above.

(Compiled by Henry E. Christiansen)

CALENDAR OF FEAST DAYS

Feast Days	1	2	3	4	5	6	7	8	9	10	11	12	13	14
Septuagesima	18 Jan.	19 Jan.	20 Jan.	21 Jan.	22 Jan.	23 Jan.	24 Jan.	25 Jan.	26 Jan.	27 Jan.	28 Jan.	29 Jan.	30 Jan.	31 Jan.
Sexagesima	25 Jan.	26 Jan.	27 Jan.	28 Jan.	29 Jan.	30 Jan.	31 Jan.	1 Feb.	2 Feb.	3 Feb.	4 Feb.	5 Feb.	6 Feb.	7 Feb.
Quinquagesima	1 Feb.	2 Feb.	3 Feb.	4 Feb.	5 Feb.	6 Feb.	7 Feb.	8 Feb.	9 Feb.	10 Feb.	11 Feb.	12 Feb.	13 Feb.	14 Feb.
Invocavit	8 Feb.	9 Feb.	10 Feb.	11 Feb.	12 Feb.	13 Feb.	14 Feb.	15 Feb.	16 Feb.	17 Feb.	18 Feb.	19 Feb.	20 Feb.	21 Feb.
Reminiscere	15 Feb.	16 Feb.	17 Feb.	18 Feb.	19 Feb.	20 Feb.	21 Feb.	22 Feb.	23 Feb.	24 Feb.	25 Feb.	26 Feb.	27 Feb.	28 Feb.
Oculi	22 Feb.	23 Feb.	24 Feb.	25 Feb.	26 Feb.	27 Feb.	28 Feb.	1 Mar.	2 Mar.	3 Mar.	4 Mar.	5 Mar.	6 Mar.	7 Mar.
Laetare	1 Mar.	2 Mar.	3 Mar.	4 Mar.	5 Mar.	6 Mar.	7 Mar.	8 Mar.	9 Mar.	10 Mar.	11 Mar.	12 Mar.	13 Mar.	14 Mar.
Judica	8 Mar.	9 Mar.	10 Mar.	11 Mar.	12 Mar.	13 Mar.	14 Mar.	15 Mar.	16 Mar.	17 Mar.	18 Mar.	19 Mar.	20 Mar.	21 Mar.
Palmarum (Palm Sunday)	15 Mar.	16 Mar.	17 Mar.	18 Mar.	19 Mar.	20 Mar.	21 Mar.	22 Mar.	23 Mar.	24 Mar.	25 Mar.	26 Mar.	27 Mar.	28 Mar.
Pascha (Satirious) (Easter)	22 Mar.	23 Mar.	24 Mar.	25 Mar.	26 Mar.	27 Mar.	28 Mar.	29 Mar.	30 Mar.	31 Mar.	1 Apr.	2 Apr.	3 Apr.	4 Apr.
Quasimodogeniti	29 Mar.	30 Mar.	31 Mar.	1 Apr.	2 Apr.	3 Apr.	4 Apr.	5 Apr.	6 Apr.	7 Apr.	8 Apr.	9 Apr.	10 Apr.	11 Apr.
Misericordias	5 Apr.	6 Apr.	7 Apr.	8 Apr.	9 Apr.	10 Apr.	11 Apr.	12 Apr.	13 Apr.	14 Apr.	15 Apr.	16 Apr.	17 Apr.	18 Apr.
Jubilate	12 Apr.	13 Apr.	14 Apr.	15 Apr.	16 Apr.	17 Apr.	18 Apr.	19 Apr.	20 Apr.	21 Apr.	22 Apr.	23 Apr.	24 Apr.	25 Apr.
Cantate	19 Apr.	20 Apr.	21 Apr.	22 Apr.	23 Apr.	24 Apr.	25 Apr.	26 Apr.	27 Apr.	28 Apr.	29 Apr.	30 Apr.	1 May	2 May
Rogate	26 Apr.	27 Apr.	28 Apr.	29 Apr.	30 Apr.	1 May	2 May	3 May	4 May	5 May	6 May	7 May	8 May	9 May
Exaudi	3 May	4 May	5 May	6 May	7 May	8 May	9 May	10 May	11 May	12 May	13 May	14 May	15 May	16 May
Pentecoste (Whitsunday)	10 May	11 May	12 May	13 May	14 May	15 May	16 May	17 May	18 May	19 May	20 May	21 May	22 May	23 May
Trinitatis	17 May	18 May	19 May	20 May	21 May	22 May	23 May	24 May	25 May	26 May	27 May	28 May	29 May	30 May
Adventis	29 Nov.	30 Nov.	1 Dec.	2 Dec.	3 Dec.	27 Nov.	28 Nov.	29 Nov.	30 Nov.	1 Dec.	2 Dec.	3 Dec.	27 Nov.	28 Nov.

NOTE: For leap years add one day to all holidays in the months of January and February.

(Compiled by Henry E. Christiansen)

CALENDAR OF FEAST DAYS

Feast Days	15	16	17	18	19	20	21	22	23	24	25	26	27	28
Septuagesima	1 Feb.	2 Feb.	3 Feb.	4 Feb.	5 Feb.	6 Feb.	7 Feb.	8 Feb.	9 Feb.	10 Feb.	11 Feb.	12 Feb.	13 Feb.	14 Feb.
Sexagesima	8 Feb.	9 Feb.	10 Feb.	11 Feb.	12 Feb.	13 Feb.	14 Feb.	15 Feb.	16 Feb.	17 Feb.	18 Feb.	19 Feb.	20 Feb.	21 Feb.
Quinquagesima	15 Feb.	16 Feb.	17 Feb.	18 Feb.	19 Feb.	20 Feb.	21 Feb.	22 Feb.	23 Feb.	24 Feb.	25 Feb.	26 Feb.	27 Feb.	28 Feb.
Invocavit	22 Feb.	23 Feb.	24 Feb.	25 Feb.	26 Feb.	27 Feb.	28 Feb.	1 Mar.	2 Mar.	3 Mar.	4 Mar.	5 Mar.	6 Mar.	7 Mar.
Reminiscere	1 Mar.	2 Mar.	3 Mar.	4 Mar.	5 Mar.	6 Mar.	7 Mar.	8 Mar.	9 Mar.	10 Mar.	11 Mar.	12 Mar.	13 Mar.	14 Mar.
Oculi	8 Mar.	9 Mar.	10 Mar.	11 Mar.	12 Mar.	13 Mar.	14 Mar.	15 Mar.	16 Mar.	17 Mar.	18 Mar.	19 Mar.	20 Mar.	21 Mar.
Laetare	15 Mar.	16 Mar.	17 Mar.	18 Mar.	19 Mar.	20 Mar.	21 Mar.	22 Mar.	23 Mar.	24 Mar.	25 Mar.	26 Mar.	27 Mar.	28 Mar.
Judica	22 Mar.	23 Mar.	24 Mar.	25 Mar.	26 Mar.	27 Mar.	28 Mar.	29 Mar.	30 Mar.	31 Mar.	1 Apr.	2 Apr.	3 Apr.	4 Apr.
Palmarum (Palm Sunday)	29 Mar.	30 Mar.	31 Mar.	1 Apr.	2 Apr.	3 Apr.	4 Apr.	5 Apr.	6 Apr.	7 Apr.	8 Apr.	9 Apr.	10 Apr.	11 Apr.
Pascha (Satirious) (Easter)	5 Apr.	6 Apr.	7 Apr.	8 Apr.	9 Apr.	10 Apr.	11 Apr.	12 Apr.	13 Apr.	14 Apr.	15 Apr.	16 Apr.	17 Apr.	18 Apr.
Quasimodogeniti	12 Apr.	13 Apr.	14 Apr.	15 Apr.	16 Apr.	17 Apr.	18 Apr.	19 Apr.	20 Apr.	21 Apr.	22 Apr.	23 Apr.	24 Apr.	25 Apr.
Misericordias	19 Apr.	20 Apr.	21 Apr.	22 Apr.	23 Apr.	24 Apr.	25 Apr.	26 Apr.	27 Apr.	28 Apr.	29 Apr.	30 Apr.	1 May	2 May
Jubilate	26 Apr.	27 Apr.	28 Apr.	29 Apr.	30 Apr.	1 May	2 May	3 May	4 May	5 May	6 May	7 May	8 May	9 May
Cantate	3 May	4 May	5 May	6 May	7 May	8 May	9 May	10 May	11 May	12 May	13 May	14 May	15 May	16 May
Rogate	10 May	11 May	12 May	13 May	14 May	15 May	16 May	17 May	18 May	19 May	20 May	21 May	22 May	23 May
Exaudi	17 May	18 May	19 May	20 May	21 May	22 May	23 May	24 May	25 May	26 May	27 May	28 May	29 May	30 May
Pentecoste (Whitsunday)	24 May	25 May	26 May	27 May	28 May	29 May	30 May	31 May	1 June	2 June	3 June	4 June	5 June	6 June
Trinitatis	31 May	1 June	2 June	3 June	4 June	5 June	6 June	7 June	8 June	9 June	10 June	11 June	12 June	13 June
Adventis	29 Nov.	30 Nov.	1 Dec.	2 Dec.	3 Dec.	27 Nov.	28 Nov.	29 Nov.	30 Nov.	1 Dec.	2 Dec.	3 Dec.	27 Nov.	28 Nov.

Table Numbers

NOTE: For leap years add one day to all holidays in the months of January and February.

(Compiled by Henry E. Christiansen)

CALENDAR OF FEAST DAYS

Feast Days	Table Numbers						
	29	30	31	32	33	34	35
Septuagesima	15 Feb.	16 Feb.	17 Feb.	18 Feb.	19 Feb.	20 Feb.	21 Feb.
Sexagesima	22 Feb.	23 Feb.	24 Feb.	25 Feb.	26 Feb.	27 Feb.	28 Feb.
Quinquagesima	1 Mar.	2 Mar.	3 Mar.	4 Mar.	5 Mar.	6 Mar.	7 Mar.
Invocavit	8 Mar.	9 Mar.	10 Mar.	11 Mar.	12 Mar.	13 Mar.	14 Mar.
Reminiscere	15 Mar.	16 Mar.	17 Mar.	18 Mar.	19 Mar.	20 Mar.	21 Mar.
Oculi	22 Mar.	23 Mar.	24 Mar.	25 Mar.	26 Mar.	27 Mar.	28 Mar.
Laetare	29 Mar.	30 Mar.	31 Mar.	1 Apr.	2 Apr.	3 Apr.	4 Apr.
Judica	5 Apr.	6 Apr.	7 Apr.	8 Apr.	9 Apr.	10 Apr.	11 Apr.
Palmarum (Palm Sunday)	12 Apr.	13 Apr.	14 Apr.	15 Apr.	16 Apr.	17 Apr.	18 Apr.
Pascha (Satirious) (Easter)	19 Apr.	20 Apr.	21 Apr.	22 Apr.	23 Apr.	24 Apr.	25 Apr.
Quasimodogeniti	26 Apr.	27 Apr.	28 Apr.	29 Apr.	30 Apr.	1 May	2 May
Misericordias	3 May	4 May	5 May	6 May	7 May	8 May	9 May
Jubilate	10 May	11 May	12 May	13 May	14 May	15 May	16 May
Cantate	17 May	18 May	19 May	20 May	21 May	22 May	23 May
Rogate	24 May	25 May	26 May	27 May	28 May	29 May	30 May
Exaudi	31 May	1 June	2 June	3 June	4 June	5 June	6 June
Pentecoste (Whitsunday)	7 June	8 June	9 June	10 June	11 June	12 June	13 June
Trinitatis	14 June	15 June	16 June	17 June	18 June	19 June	20 June
Adventis	29 Nov.	30 Nov.	1 Dec.	2 Dec.	3 Dec.	27 Nov.	28 Nov.

NOTE: For leap years add one day to all holidays in the months of January and February.

(Compiled by Henry E. Christiansen)

INSTRUCTIONS FOR DETERMINING DATE OF
MOVABLE FEAST DAYS

To find the date of a Movable Feast Day in a given year:

1. Determine whether the Julian or the Gregorian Calendar was being used in the country under consideration. Normally, all recording in England, Wales, Ireland and British Possessions prior to 1st January 1752 and in Scotland before 1600 used the Julian Calendar.

2. Determine which Calendar Number to use by referring to the table "Guide for Finding the Date of Movable Feast Days." Locate on this table the year desired. For example, if the year was 1666 and the record used the Julian style of recording, it would be necessary to refer to Table 25 on the "Calendar of Feast Days." Thus, in that year 1666, Easter Sunday was the 15th of April. This now makes it possible to determine a proper date for a christening recorded as Easter Sunday 1666.

In a further example, suppose the date in a record is given as the Wednesday following Septuagesima Sunday, 1532. The Julian Calendar was in use in England and Wales at that time. The "Guide for Finding the Date of Movable Feast Days" shows the Table Number of 1532 as 10, but a footnote indicates that 1532 was a leap year. From the "Calendar of Feast Days," Table #10, we learn that Septuagesima Sunday was normally on the 27th of January, but since 1532 was a leap year, one day must be added to all dates falling in January and February. Consequently, Septuagesima Sunday in 1532 was on 28th January. The Wednesday following 28th January would be the 31st of January, which is the date sought.

SHORT LIST OF BOOKS
FOR DETAILED STUDY AND REFERENCE

Cappelli, A.: *Dizionario delle Abbreviature Latine ed Italiane*, (4th edn. Milan: 1949), Abbreviations.

Cheney, C. R. (Editor): *Handbook of Dates for Students of English History*, (1948).

Denholm-Young, N.: *Handwriting in England and Wales*, (Cardiff: University of Wales: 1954). Includes fascimilies and a few transcripts.

Fairbank, A.: *A Book of Scripts*, (King Penguin, 1949).

Greg, W. W.: *English Literary Autographs*, 1550-1650 (1925-32). Facsimiles, transcripts and notes.

Grieve, H. E. P.: *Examples of English Handwriting*, 1150-1750 (Essex County Council: 1954). Facsimiles and transcripts from Essex official, ecclesiastical, estate and family archives of the 12th to the 17th century.

Heal, A.: *The English Writing Masters and their Copy-books*, 1570-1800, (Cambridge: 1931). Introduction on scripts by Stanley Morison.

Hector, L. C.: *The Handwriting of English Documents*, (London: Edward Arnold, 1958). Includes facsimiles and transcripts.

Jenkinson, H.: *The Later Court Hands in England, from the 15th to the 17th Century*, (Cambridge University Press: 1927). Includes illustrated sections on different hands, methods of abbreviation and special signs, numerals, punctuation, etc. Writing Masters' alphabets, facsimilies and transcripts. Bibliography.

Johnson, C., and Jenkinson, H.: *English Court Hand, A.D. 1066 to 1500:* (Oxford: 1915). Includes sections on evolution of court hand, writing materials, methods of abbreviation, common abbreviations; illustrates forms of individual letters, special signs, numerals, punctuation, etc., at different dates. Facsimiles and transcripts. Bibliography.

Johnson, C., and Jenkinson, H.: *Medieval Latin Word List*, (Oxford: 1934; re-issued 1947).

Judge, C. B.: *Specimens of Sixteenth Century English Handwriting*, (Harvard: 1935). Notes on methods of abbreviation. Writing Masters' alphabets and facsimiles but no transcripts. Bibliography.

Martin, C. T.: *The Record Interpreter* (2nd edn. 1910). Abbreviations; glossary of Latin words; Latin forms of names.

McKerrow, R. B.: "The Capital Letters in Elizabethan Handwriting," in *Rev. of Eng. Studies*, Vol. iii, (1927) No. 9. (Reprint).

Powicke, F. M. (Editor): *Handbook of British Chronology*, (Royal Historical Society: 1939).

Schulz, H. C.: "The Teaching of Handwriting in Tudor and Stuart Times," in *Huntington Library Quarterly*, VI (1943), 381-425.

Thompson, Sir E. M.: *Introduction to Greek and Latin Palaeography*, (Oxford: 1912). Includes facsimiles and transcripts.

Tschichold, J.: *An Illustrated History of Writing and Lettering*, (1947).

Wright, A.: *Court Hand Restored*, (London: 1773, 1818 and other editions).

Wright, C. E.: *English Vernacular Hands from the Twelfth to the Fifteenth Centuries*, (Oxford: The Clarendon Press: 1960).

LATIN:

Baxter, J., *Medieval Latin Word List*, (Oxford: 1947).

Beeson, C. H.: *Primer of Medieval Latin*, (Chicago: 1926).

Gooder, E. A.: *Latin for Local History*, (London: Longmans, Green & Co: 1961).

"Report on editing historical documents," in *Bulletin of the Institute of Historical Research*, (London: 1925), vol. 1. Rules for making an accurate transcript.

British Records Association: *Notes for the Guidance of Editors of Record Publications* (1946). Rules for transcribing.

In addition, for most areas there are books to help with purely local difficulties, such as place and field-names, dialect words, etc.

SECTION TWO

CHAPTER 9

Research Standards

By comparison with that found in other countries genealogical connections in England and Wales are among the most difficult to demonstrate. This is partly because of difficulties in obtaining access to and searching genealogical records, but mainly because of the limited amount of information recorded in them.

In some European countries in past centuries, families were not free to move from place to place without first stating their intention and registering with the government officials concerned as to where they were going and from whence they came. The resulting records of these family checks and movements have been a boon to genealogists.

Generally, this was not the case in England and Wales, as apart from certain restrictions imposed by the Poor Laws, individuals were free to come and go as they pleased without a specific record of these movements being made. This makes genealogical research into all but the wealthy families very difficult.

Unless an ancestral family or their relatives had interests in lands, houses, or other property, usually there was nothing recorded in land records or probate court grants. These factors, along with common given names and surnames, make it difficult to determine correct pedigree connections. There are methods that can be used to identify our ancestors, however, and the purpose of this chapter is to describe the procedures and standards that should be used in this identification.

Importance of Background

Before research commences, it is necessary for the researcher to become familiar with the economic, political, social and historic background of the country, the county, and the specific locality. The use and repetition, locally and by families, of unusual given names; the commonness or uniqueness of surnames; the customs of the towns and villages; the employment opportunities at various periods of time — these must all be considered. The solution of a research problem and an appreciation of the chance of finding ancestral connections is in fact often dependent upon an understanding of factors such as the following:

    i. The movements of population caused by the agrian revolution and by government control of agriculture and wages.

    ii. The movements of population caused by people seeking employment in the industries that resulted from the Industrial Revolution; movements caused by increase of business and the failure of commercial endeavors.

   iii. Child mortality, pestilences, and plagues.

   iv. Wars and civil disturbances.

   v. Migrations and emigrations.

   vi. Topography and geography.

   vii. Affiliation with various religious denominations who maintained their own records.

Recording of Information

It is necessary from the very outset of research to file recorded information in a well planned and orderly manner so that the results can be studied with ease and speed. Suggestions made by others might be adapted to individual needs as long as they are both efficient and time-saving. Any method of recording must adequately identify the sources used. The secret of organizing material is in the arranging of the pedigree lines by locality and surnames,[1] and filing the research results in the same way.[2]

The copying of the complete entry, exactly as found in the original source, is essential. No attempt should be made at "on the spot" displacement or alteration of entries or division into families. Abbreviations are permissable but should be used with caution — they are time-saving if they are consistent and used with prudence. For example, Jno., Geo., and Eliza might mean John, George, and Eliza, but to another person they might be interpreted as Jonathan, Geoffrey, and Elizabeth.

The type of record being used should also be noted, such as christening (baptism), marriage, burial (death), tombstone inscription, etc. It is impossible to arrive at any satisfactory conclusion if there is any doubt as to how the original record read.[3]

Copy dates as found, but clearly state in your notes that the dates recorded are as found. Be certain to note whether the clerk was consistent. There are instances where the ecclesiastical year was used and also the historical year. If this is not noted it may not be possible, in later analysis, to know what year was intended. It is not incorrect to use double dating if that will assist in the identification of dates copied, but normally, dates recorded in the style of the ecclesiastical year that commenced on Lady Day, the 25th of March, should be recorded as written.[4]

Bear the change of calendar in mind, however, when tabulating the research notes into family groups[5] and evaluating a research problem.

---

[1]See *Genealogical Research in England and Wales*, V. 2, chap. 1, and D. Harland, *Research Standards*, Chap. 18 "Listing Sources of Information."

[2]See *Genealogical Research in England and Wales*, V. 2, chap. 1.

[3]*Ibid*, v. 1, pp. 184-185.

[4]See *Genealogical Research in England and Wales*, v. 1, pp. 159-160.

[5]See *Genealogical Instruction Manual*, section 3, pp. 70-71.

It is possible that in both original and microfilmed records pages may have been torn out, or missed during microfilming. Therefore watch for page continuity.[6]

Original and Printed Sources

Whether original sources, transcripts, or printed books are being searched, read all introductions and prefaces completely.[7] If there are several volumes in the series, read the introductions in *each* volume. Important details concerning the methods of transcription, the customs of the locality, and the families recorded, may be given there. Publications often embrace only the early records as a vast amount of work is yet to be done by transcribers. If the period relating to the searcher's pedigree problem has not been transcribed or printed, recourse to the originals is necessary. The introductions and prefaces, however, relating to the earlier periods in print should be read carefully, however, because they often give excellent information about the later records.

Do not depend entirely upon statements found on title pages. Even printed books have misleading titles. Study the text to determine whether the record is complete for the period stated or whether only extracts and abstracts, and not the complete record, have been transcribed.[8]

Record the title and volume number, the author or editor (if any), the library call number (if any), and other positive information identifying the source. The periods searched, with details of years (or parts of years) that are missing or illegible, must be recorded.[9]

Indexes are to be used with care. Some are unreliable and contain errors, omissions, and spelling anomalies. If the index does not disclose the information required, search the lists of entries and the text for the period involved.[10]

Typographical errors and omissions (*corrigenda, addenda and errata*) may be listed in the volume concerned or in a *later* volume of the same series.[11]

It is stressed that the ability to read original records must be developed. Those who have transcribed ancient records are not aware of the pedigree connections so well known to the family genealogist. Since the transcriber may misinterpret the spelling of a surname or a

---

[6]Op. cit. v. 1, pp. 184, 201-202.
[7]Op. cit. v. 1, pp. 220-226, v. 2, pp. 71-72, 92-93.
[8]*Ibid:* v. 1, pp. 177-178 for incorrect title pages, and pp. 223-224 for incomplete records.
[9]*Ibid:* v. 1, p. 202 for recording inconsistent records and missing years.
[10]*Ibid:* v. 1, pp. 179-182 for examples of spelling, and p. 179 for incorrect transcription of surnames that would be impossible to identify in an index.
[11]*Ibid:* v. 2, p. 72.

place, it is well worth while to search the originals and discover the correct rendering of a family name which may have been incorrectly copied into the transcribed or printed version.

Census Records[12]

The 1841 and later census returns *should always be searched* for contemporary families even though other genealogical records existing for the same period have also been searched.

All census records prepared during the child-bearing lifetime of the mother of the children should be searched, and also when possible and practical, a ten- or twenty-year period following, for the place or places at which the family resided. These searches may disclose additional children born in a family but not disclosed in searches made in the other contemporary records. The 1851 census and later returns usually show ages and places of birth, and are thus valuable in strengthening information found in other records. These returns may also disclose information on visiting relatives as well as clues to the identity of children born out of wedlock.

Census returns should always be searched for record of direct ancestors, if it is known or suspected that they were alive at that time, in order that ages and places of birth can be found. They should also be used to support or question possible connections made from searches in other records.

After searches in church records and probate records, comparison with entries appearing in a contemporary census may identify brothers and sisters and their families, witnesses and in-laws, thus opening for study the collateral branches of a family.

Civil Registration of Births, Marriages and Deaths since 1 July 1837

These records *are* to be used in conjunction with the census records, church records and probate records in order to complete family groups. The birth, marriage and death certificates of direct ancestors *should always be obtained*. These may provide additional pedigree information or verify unproven information already in the possession of the family. A decision should be made to obtain "long form" birth certificates for other members of a family group if it becomes necessary to check on possible differences in the recording of names, caused perhaps because of mis-hearing, misunderstanding, and poor handwriting.[13] After a search of post-1837 burial registers,[14] in church records and cemeteries, there may be found records of persons who are not fully identified. The corresponding death certificates from the local register

---

[12]*Ibid:* v. 1, pp. 84-117
[13]*Ibid:* v. 1, pp. 73-80
[14]*Ibid:* v. 1, p. 153 shows illustration of the brief information found in burial registers.

office or from the Registrar General at Somerset House, London, may clearly identify the deceased.[15]

Church Records

There include the parish registers of the Established Church of England and the Bishop's Transcripts of those parish registers, and registers of the various Nonconformist denominations,[16] including the Society of Friends (Quakers), the Roman Catholics, the Jews, and a few foreign groups such as the Huguenots.[17]

After a short search establishing a probable pedigree connection in church records, it is necessary to make general searches, listing *all* entries of the surname involved for the periods searched. This is necessary because evaluation of evidence found in church records is usually based upon comparison, thus making it essential to copy all entries of the pedigree surnames.

When a marriage entry on the direct line is found in a *printed* or other copied parish register or obtained from the pre-1813 Bishop's Transcripts, a copy of the *complete* entry must be obtained from the *original* register or its microfilm copy. The original is sometimes more complete than the copies. Printed and other copies of marriage entries and marriage indexes are known to have errors and omissions, therefore a negative search in them does not necessarily mean that the marriage is not recorded in the *original.*

From 1754 to at least 1837 a check must be made to discover whether the banns books of a given parish have survived.[18] These should be searched for references to the "intention to marry" of ancestors and collateral relatives who married in another parish church or parochial chapelry.

When a pre-1837 marriage entry in a parish register or Bishop's Transcript indicates that the marriage took place by *license*, the marriage bond and marriage allegation should be sought for the additional genealogical information usually available there.[19]

The splendid series of Boyd's *Marriage Indexes* provides a short cut in an attempt to locate a marriage. The researcher must beware of errors and omissions and should realize that these important indexes do *not* cover all marriages in any given parish or county. Mr. Boyd

---

[15]*Ibid:* v. 1, pages 57 and 59
[16]*Ibid:* v. 1, chaps. 15, 16, and 17
[17]*Ibid:* v. 1, chap 15
[18]*Ibid:* v. 1, pp. 149-150, 206-211
[19]*Ibid:* v. 1, pp. 211-217, v. 2, p. 204, and v. 2, chap. 9, lists all printed copies of licenses.

used only those marriage registers which were *available to him for varying periods.*[20]

Bishop's Transcripts are a valuable source and are usually more accessible than non-copied parish registers. For this reason they are often searched to establish pedigree connections, but they should be used with prudence. Accurate lists of years or parts of years missing or illegible must be kept in order that one may check the *original* registers and so fill the gaps.[21] Even when the Bishop's Transcripts are complete for lengthy pre-1813 periods, a spot-check of the original parish registers should be made for christenings, marriages, and burials of the family of a direct ancestor. When this check discloses that the Bishop's Transcripts are an abbreviated version of the parish registers it is necessary to search the parish register completely.

After the introduction of Lord Hardwicke's Marriage Act in 1754 some ministers did not record marriage entries on the Bishop's Transcript copy of their parish registers.

In *all instances* the registers of the Nonconformist denominations in a wide area must be searched, including the records of the Society of Friends (Quakers) and the Roman Catholics (in strong Catholic areas). There also existed in London from 1742 to 1837 a Registry of the Presbyterians, Independents (Congregationalists) and Baptists, and from 1818 to 1837 a Registry of the Wesleyan Methodists containing records mainly from London localities with some birth records from ministers in various parts of England.

The records of the Jews should also be considered when there is a family connection in or near a Jewish community.

These records are to be checked because a family could have attended church in more than one denomination during a lifetime, adherents were willing to travel long distances in order to worship as they chose, and their ministers travelled wide circuits.[22]

Probate Records

Before 11 January 1858, the great majority of probates were granted in the *ecclesiastical courts* by officials appointed by the Church of England. The course of action on the part of executors or next-of-kin generally was determined by the location of the deceased's prop-

---

[20]*Ibid:* v. 2, pp. 201-203, and chap. 9. See also *A Key to Boyd's Marriage Index* (London: The Society of Genealogists, 1963), 2nd ed., but the listings in the booklet are incomplete. A reasonably accurate listing of all the parishes and periods involved is in the Library, The Genealogical Society, Salt Lake City.

[21]*Ibid:* v. 1, chap. 13, and particularly page 202.

[22]*Ibid:* v. 1, pp. 239-253, for the whereabouts of Nonconformist registers and the Registries in London. The records formerly kept at the General Register Office, Somerset House, London, are now transferred to the Public Record Office, Chancery Lane, London. The Jews are mentioned in Chapter 16, and Roman Catholics in Chapter 17.

erty. Record searchers rarely know where the property was located, therefore it is necessary to proceed by searching the probate records of the smallest jurisdiction and extending the search to the higher jurisdictions.[23] Adjoining jurisdictions should be considered, as members of the family may have moved to a nearby place which was within a different jurisdiction.[24]

Searches in probate records should not be confined to the finding of the Will or Administration of a particular individual. After an initial search to find a particular record, all Wills and Administrations of a given family surname in a given period and area should be read to help complete family group records and extend the pedigree. The fact that a person is known or stated to be poor should not preclude a researcher from using probate records. Grants of probate and letters of administration are to be found for paupers, laborers, weavers, and others of humble circumstances. Persons of little or no estate are to be found mentioned in the Wills of their wealthier relatives.

Success will often be possible in the proving of connections for an ancestress, even when only *her* maiden name and surname are known, and none of her brothers', sisters', or parents' names are known. In instances in which parents lived after the marriage of their daughters, and if the daughters are mentioned by their married name in a parent's probate record there is little doubt as to their identity in relation to their husband and their parentage. This is also true when the probate record identifies married sisters of the deceased and names their husbands. These same sisters may well be mentioned in their parent's probate record as *unmarried* children who are now clearly identified by a brother's or sister's probate record. In the case of male ancestors, however, the fact that a person bearing the same given and surname as an ancestor is mentioned in a probate record is not proof that this reference relates to the person on the pedigree unless there are supporting facts, such as name of other family members or recognizable in-laws.

Wills, and sometimes Administrations, disclose names of children, brothers and sisters, and other close kin not found mentioned in church records. In contrast to this, there was no legal requirement that a testator mention all or any members of his family, and the Letters of Administration of an intestate might name only one person — the next-of-kin. Several sources must therefore be used to provide correct and complete information about a family.

Other Sources

Those already cited are the most commonly used sources of genealogical information. All other sources, and there are many, extant for

[23]*Ibid:* v. 2, pp. 39-48
[24]*Ibid:* v. 2, pp. 51-52

the period of the pedigree problem should be considered and searched as far as may be necessary. Some of these sources are military records, Quarter Sessions, Poor Law Records, Feet of Fines, Manor Court Rolls, etc.

Obstructions in the Way of Research Progress

There may be good reasons why unsuccessful searches have been made for birth, christening, marriage, death, and burial entries in either Civil Registration or in church records. Some of these include:

i. *Erroneous information in the possession of the searcher,* perhaps based on previous, but poor, research, the lack of proper evaluation of the evidence, and the failure to adequately test family traditions.[25]

ii. *Incorrect names and places entered in official records,* some given in error, some in good faith, and others through perjury.[26]

iii. *Spelling of names* as known to the researcher may be different from that found in the records. Indexes in the General Register Office and those found in parish registers may carry the entry sought but under a spelling entirely unknown to the searcher. This may be attributed to phonetic spelling, accent, mis-hearing or bad handwriting.[27]

iv. *Illiterate recordings* for a surname in ancient church records are not always recognized — even by specialists.[28]

v. *A surname of a child is often hidden,* either by the parent or the child. If the parent registers the child, it may be in a surname entirely unknown to the searcher. The child's mother might have married shortly after its birth and not informed her child of her unwed condition at the time of its birth. As her maiden surname might be unknown, a search for the birth record of the child would be impossible. Occasionally children born in wedlock are correctly registered, but their mother, marrying again, has them reared in the surname of her second husband.[29]

---

[25] A record searcher in a signed report dated 1936 claimed that Thomas Humphery who died 9 August 1868 at Sutton in Ashfield and was a former resident of Mansfield and Skegby, all nearby places in Nottinghamshire, was the same person who had been christened at Skegby 9 Sept. 1783. This pedigree had then been extended ten generations back to 1495. A later search disclosed that this Thomas Humphery was recorded in the 1851 Census, aged 64 years, born in Blackwell, Derbyshire, where there is a christening 3 May 1786 for Thomas son of Thomas and Ann Humphery.

[26] op. cit. v. 1, pp. 48, 64, 82.

[27] *Ibid:* v. 1, pp. 65 to 68, 179 to 180, 275. See "widows" on p. 61 and 66.

[28] *Ibid:* v. 1, pp. 176 for misinterpretations, pp. 179-180 for unusual spellings.

[29] *Ibid:* v. 1, pp. 72-73. Elizabeth Carver was aged 11 in 1861. It is impossible to find her birth record under this name. In 1851 she is Elizabeth Votier age 1 year, and was registered under this name, her parents being married. Her mother, Elizabeth Votier, later married George Carver, hence the description in 1861 is misleading.

General Notes

If searches in all the principal and primary sources, some of which have been described above and other contemporary records that might help *have failed to supply direct evidence* for the acceptance of a pedigree connection, it is necessary to attempt to resolve the problem in another way. This is done by an evaluation and analysis of the information obtained from extensive 'area' searches using correctly established research procedures.

The solution might be possible by the use of circumstantial evidence which require a certain amount of inference and calculation to arrive at the required conclusion. As the research listings are analyzed, special attention is needed to detect conflicting evidence, which in turn will make any conclusion based solely on inference and calculation unacceptable until the conflicts are acceptably removed.

If there is no conflicting evidence, and all extant records have been properly searched as described later, and if all the circumstantial evidence is examined and found to fit the case, the pedigree connection can then be said to have been "circumstantially proved beyond reasonable doubt."

CHAPTER TEN

Research Procedures

In order to provide information on research procedures which involve all necessary efforts to build a strong case of circumstantial evidence, the following SITUATIONS are offered, *assuming always that all necessary sources have been used and do not provide the supporting direct evidence required.*

It is recommended that *all* the situations be studied carefully before searches are made, as a particular research problem may contain parts of several of these situations. The rules given are valuable and are based on many years of experience.

PROCEDURE NUMBER ONE

A census record, family record, or other reliable source, provides for a particular individual an age at a dated event and a birthplace. ONE PROBABLE BIRTH OR CHRISTENING RECORD HAS BEEN FOUND IN A CHURCH RECORD FOR THIS INDIVIDUAL. THE NAMES OF THE PARENTS OF THIS ANCESTOR ARE NOT KNOWN TO THE PRESENT GENERATION.

Note that this is a situation where the parentage is not known, but there will be instances where the name of one or both parents are known. This information will lend weight when a record is found for a child who has a given name corresponding to that of one of the parents and this should be borne in mind as the problem is considered.

The census returns for 1851 and later record an age and a birthplace, usually a parish and county, for each person. A family record, such as an old Family Bible, might supply an age or a birth date and a birthplace. A military record might supply an age and birthplace for a serviceman.

For example a family record might record that John Smallwood was born 6 July 1812 at Battle, Sussex

OR

an 1851 census return might state that John Smallwood was aged 38, born in Battle, Sussex

OR

an 1830 Army Muster Roll might state that John Smallwood was aged 18, born at Battle, Sussex.

The parish registers of Battle may show the following entry:

Chr. 10 August 1812 John son of Robert and Mary Smallwood.

This entry cannot be accepted as ancestral at this point, even supposing that all three pieces of information listed above had been known instead of one. The reason for not accepting this entry at once will become apparent as the next few pages are studied. The objective of those pages could be summarized as follows:

1. How correct is the information given?

2. Can I find any likely alternative entries in the area?

3. Can I find any conflicting evidence in the area?

Having found in the parish registers of the town, city or ecclesiastical parish covering the *stated birthplace,*[30] only *one* probably christening or birth record agreeing (within a year or two) with a *calculated or stated year of birth,* the following procedures are necessary to either strengthen or eliminate the acceptance of this circumstantial evidence:

i. If possible and practical, confirm the calculated or stated year of birth and stated birthplace by finding record of the same person in at least two census returns. For example, the 1861 census returns may confirm Battle as the birthplace of John Smallwood or, as sometimes happens, give a *different* place of birth.

ii. If possible and practical, the census of the stated place of birth should be searched to determine whether there are other persons of the same name, age and birthplace living there who might be confused with the likely candidate already found. Consideration should be given to similar searches in the census of other parishes within a five mile radius of the stated place of birth. (See the Enderby example on pages 93-97 of *Genealogical Research in England and Wales,* Vol. 1, showing how two men named William Enderby living in separate parishes when the census was taken were both born in the same place in the same year.)

iii. Consider ages given at as many dated events as possible to see if they agree as to the year of birth of the ancestor. If there is a wide variance, consider the possibility that the *earlier* recordings, that is, the recordings nearest to the year of birth, will probably be the most correct.

iv. Make sure that the search in the christening or birth records that disclosed the entry was for a period five year earlier than the calculated or stated year of birth and up to at least the year that the known relative married. Sometimes persons are christened just prior to their marriage, but to be identified, the entry must specify a birth date, age, "adult", or "of riper years."[31]

v. Burial records must be searched to determine whether the person named in the christening entry entry either died as an infant or

---

[30]See *Genealogical Research in England and Wales,* v. 1, pp. 118-122 and 164-166.
[31]*Ibid.,* v. 1, pp. 186-187, "Riper years"

survived to marriageable age or later.[32] Efforts should be made to discover whether a new parish was created and a churchyard opened later than 1813 that might have registers recording the burials of families whose christening records are in the registers of the *old* parish church.[33]

Some parish ministers served two (and sometimes more) parishes, and occasionally recorded in the register of one parish events that took place in another.[34]

The Church of England did not enforce any rule as to where a child was to be christened, thus parents were at liberty to have children christened by any parish minister who was conveniently situated as far as the child was concerned.

Sometimes a christening involved an urgent call upon the nearest available parish minister or curate to baptize "privately" an infant who was thought to be near death. The event might well be recorded in a neighboring parish, or forgotten and not registered.

Parents who resided in one parish might take a child across the parish boundary to a conveniently situated parish church, because their own parish church was at some distance. The neighboring parish church might be only a matter of a few hundred yards away.[35]

vi. Searches should be made for alternative christening or birth entries in the registers of all the Church of England parishes that *adjoin*[36] or surround the parish where the birth is said to have taken place, until all parishes within a minimum of a five mile radius have been searched. If any of these parishes have registers missing for the period needed, the search of the area has not been made.

In *addition* to the searching of these parishes the following should be taken into consideration:

a. The geographical and topographical features of the area. Wide rivers without bridges, or long, narrow, inhabited mountain valley, etc., may modify the procedure.

b. Ancestral connections with military installations such as dockyards, naval bases, army barracks, etc., may require an extension of the five mile radius. Such an ancestor could have been christened at one such installation having been born many miles away at another.

---

[32]*Ibid.*, v. v, pp. 95-96, shows that two children, both named William Enderby were born in the same parish only four months apart. Both survived childhood, were married, became parents of children, and were both found recorded in the 1851 census returns.

[33]*Ibid.*, v. 1, pp. 36, 142-143, 193-194

[34]This situation is sometimes detectable when a reference book states that a parish is "annexed to" or "consolidated with" or "a chapelry of" another parish.

[35]*Ibid.*, v. 1, p. 121, and v. 2, for maps on pp. 358-359, 366-367, 410-411, 414-415.

[36]Depending on localities and occupations.

c. Parishes or towns with associated occupations should be included in the search if the ancestral occupation is known and

if it is a specialized one. For example, Frome in Somerset and Trowbridge in Wiltshire were famous for their manufacture of woolen cloth. They are about ten miles apart and both are surrounded by small agricultural parishes. An ancestor whose family followed this occupation should certainly be searched for in both towns.

It is stressed that the period to be searched should be five years before the earliest calculated or stated year of birth right up to the year the ancestor married, searches being made in both the christening and burial registers. When the marriage date of the ancestor is not known, use the year in which the first known child was born or christened.

d. Some ecclesiastical parishes in heavily populated *industrial areas* are several miles in area, containing many townships, the inhabitants frequenting *one* parish church. In those cases the registers of those parishes that *adjoin* should be searched.

e. The economic situation of the area and the period of time should also be considered. The failure of a coal mine, the sinking of a coal mine, the building of a factory, low farm wages, the movement of people because of the industrial and agrarian revolutions, such factors should all be carefully considered.

vii. The marriage registers of the stated place of birth and of the parishes that adjoin and surround should be searched to determine whether a person or persons of that name can be "married off" to someone other than the person to whom the ancestor is known to have married. The period to be searched in the marriage registers should begin fifteen years after the christening of the likely candidate and extend up to 40 years after.

viii. In the case of a male ancestor, careful watch should be kept for the possibility of a person bearing the same given name and surname having children christened in the parish in which the claimed ancestor is said to have been born *at the same time* as the ancestor was having children born or christened in that parish or elsewhere. Watch also for the probability that the male person found christened in one parish can be eliminated as the ancestral connection by finding record of *his* children born or christened in a *nearby* parish.

For example, John Smallwood is stated to have been born at Battle and a likely birth or christening has been found there. Is there a John Smallwood having children there a generation later who could be this John Smallwood? Or are there *two* John Smallwood's having children there a generation later? Or is there a John Smallwood having children nearby, a generation later, who could be the one born or christened at Battle in 1812?

ix. Irrespective of the supposed or known religious belief of an ances-tor, the registers of the Church of England and the registers of all Nonconformist chapels (including Quakers), and the Roman Catholics, where available covering the *area*, should be searched for the essential periods. The area in which all Nonconformist chapels should be considered will be determined by geographical and topographical conditions, but as a general rule, a minimum of a ten mile radius should be used.[37] This is because persons with strong beliefs were prepared to travel long distances to wor-ship, and some Nonconformists kept "circuit" registers that record children born in a parish many miles from the place of registra-tion. In the case of Quakers, it is wise to search the records of the monthly and quarterly meetings that adjoin and surround the claimed ancestral place of residence.[38]

Breaches in the faithful attendance at the usual church or chapel are rarely mentioned in family tradition, but there are on record many instances where unsuspected nonconformity has been un-covered through the use of these standards.

x. When Bishop's Transcripts are used, the missing and illegible per-iods *must* be searched in the parish registers. The ideal is to search both these sources completely.

xi. The search for a birth or christening record under a known sur-name might fail should the ancestor have been born out of wedlock and recorded in the surname of his single or widowed mother (a surname probably unknown to the searcher) and then reared under another surname. Such a situation would call for a listing in the supposed place of birth (all demonimations to be included) for a determined period, the list to include all children of the same given name, irrespective of surname.

A comparison should then be made with marriages and burials that took place after the birth of these children in an endeavor to determine whether:

a. A woman bearing an illegitimate child married shortly after-wards and the child grew up under his father's (if the mother married his father) or his step-father's (if the mother married another man) surname. Here is an actual example:

The 1851 census shows THOMAS SLOAN, age 40, born St. Bees, a large parish containing the town of Whitehaven, Cum-berland. He had children named Elizabeth and Edward. He

---

[37]*See* footnote 22.

[38]The records of the Society of Friends or Quakers are easily accessible at the **Public** Record Office, London, and at the Library of the Society of Friends, London. **They** are, however, not in parish order, but are arranged in returns of meetings **each** covering large areas sometimes for several counties. The Preparative Meeting was **the** local meeting, a Monthly Meeting usually consisting of several preparative meetings, and a Quarterly meeting of a number of monthly meetings.

was married before 1837. Family records list a younger brother Edward Sloan of Whitehaven, but no date of birth. No Thomas Sloan christening was found around 1810 in the registers of St. Bees, St. Nicholas, St. James, or Holy Trinity, Whitehaven. A number of children named Thomas were found recorded, including a christening in 1810 for Thomas, son of Elizabeth Fisher. In 1814 an Edward Sloan, mariner, married Elizabeth Fisher. In 1817 Edward, son of Edward and Elizabeth Sloan, mariner, was christened. It appears clear that Thomas was born in 1810, his mother married in 1814, and *he was reared in the surname of Sloan,* and his younger brother was born in 1817.

b. A married woman bears a child about the time of her husband's death. If she married again shortly afterwards, the child could have grown up under either his father's or his step-father's surname.

xii. It is not often possible to detect *naming customs* among English and Welsh families. It is possible that parents named their children after themselves or their own parents, but this cannot be detected unless the given names used are unusual and uncommon. It is not enough to discover a pattern with given names such as William, Thomas, Elizabeth and Mary, etc., because of their frequent occurence generally.

There is the possibility, however, that the use of unusual and uncommon names can be detected through several generations. If this is obvious, it will strengthen the acceptance of a particular family as ancestral. Care should be taken, however, to understand what is an uncommon or unusual given name. Before this can be assumed, a study of the given names used in the area in other parishes must be made.

For example, in the industrial area of the West Riding of Yorkshire, biblical names are common. In this area, therefore names like Solomon, Nathaniel, Abednego, etc., could not be considered uncommon, whereas they *are* uncommon in other areas. The female given name Wilmot is uncommon in most areas but is common in Cornwall. In some instances a surname is used as a first given name. For example, John Smith married Mary Field.

It is possible that one of the children could be given the name Field as a given name. The practice is more common in some parts of the country than others and such a name is usually given to a male child.

Research evaluation should also take into consideration the matter of persons with compound names such as Mary Ann, using only one of them or being listed in a record under only one of them.

It is possible that a person christened Mary Ann might have married as Mary and be listed as Ann when her children were christened.

The 1841 census enumerators were instructed to record only one of the given names for any individual, thus a boy listed as William in that census could have been recorded at birth as Alfred William.[39] There are certain names that may be synonymous in certain families or certain localities. A girl christened Sarah may have been married as Sally, Peggy as Margaret, Ann as Hannah, but careful evaluation is needed as no definite rule applied.

xiii.   Where other "conflicting" birth or christening entries are found in other records within the prescribed area, attempts should be made to find what happened to each individual. The usual procedures of checking the burials and marriages should be followed. It may be possible to "bury off" or "marry off" these persons, and these attempts should be made throughout a five mile radius of the place *where these* persons were born or christened rather than where the possible ancestor is known to have been born or christened. Even though the probate records had been unsuccessfully searched in an attempt to prove if the person found originally is ancestral, it may still be possible to search them and prove that the other conflicting entries found can be accounted for or ruled out, thereby clearing that obstruction. It is always easier to prove the female connections through probate records than it is to prove a male connection. This is because a married girl is usually recorded in her married surname.

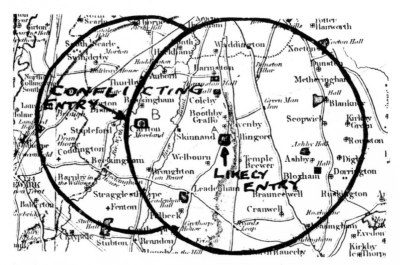

Parish A is the supposed place of birth of the ancestor, and a likely birth or christening has been found there. In the search for alternative christenings that would conflict, all places within a five mile radius have been searched. A conflicting entry has been found in parish B. Attempts must be made to eliminate this by searching all parishes within the broken circle.

---

[39]*Ibid.*, v. 1, p. 61, William Mead example.

PROCEDURE NUMBER TWO

A census or other record states a place of birth and an age for a particular individual, but no parentage. MORE THAN ONE POSSIBLE BIRTH OR CHRISTENING ENTRY HAS BEEN FOUND IN THAT PLACE.

Even though possible christenings have been found recorded in the stated place of birth, the searching of adjoining parishes, as described in Procedure Number 1 should be followed. The christenings or birth entries likely to be ancestral should be within a year or two of the calculated year of birth. When a child is not christened until after one year of age, an age at christening might be given, making it still possible to calculate the year of birth. Sometimes family records give a date of birth. Although this date may be wrong, parts of that date of birth often coincide with an actual birth or christening record that has been found and consideration should be given to this. For example:

Family Record	*Original Source*
5 May 1821	5 June 1821
5 May 1821	5 May 1822
5 May 1821	6 May 1821

Dates in letters from Europe such as 1/11/1821 (1 November 1821) can be misinterpreted to be January 11, 1821.

The search of burial and marriage registers described in Situation #1 might eliminate one or more of the possible ancestral entries.

It is always important to make every effort to find the marriage and the subsequent children of the children of every candidate. In this manner it is often possible to determine what happened to each candidate. A probate record could mention one or more of the likely candidates and eliminate them even though they are not ancestral.

If more than one entry is left and efforts in all other sources have failed to clarify the situation, one should consider that those likely candidates remaining *may have ancestry in common* and have a cousin relationship. Attempts should be made to find trace of the ancestry of these persons to determine whether they have common ancestry converging in an earlier generation. If they do, then they have common ancestry on the male side, although it will not be possible to prove the lines of the mothers of those cousins or second cousins. For example, Daniel Todd died September 1846 age 76, therefore he was born around 1770. He was born at Eye, Suffolk. The parish registers of Eye, Suffolk, disclose christening entries for 13 May 1770, Daniel, son of Joseph Todd, and 7 July 1771, Daniel son of John Todd. Both survived infancy and subsequently married. Which one was the ancestor? All sources failed to differentiate between the two children. The ancestry of both was traced in Eye, and their fathers, Joseph and John, were found to be brothers, sons of John Todd who married in 1731 to Elizabeth Pretty.

On the other hand, two boys named Robert Brind were christened at Aldbourne, Wiltshire, and either one of these boys could be ancestral. The above described procedure was followed, and it was possible to develop the Brind line of each of them back to the beginning of the registers in 1637 *without the line converging.*

If all efforts fail and more than one likely entry is still available, then the ancestor cannot be determined, and the ancestral line is halted at that point.

PROCEDURE NUMBER THREE

A census or other record lists an age and birthplace of an individual, but no parentage. NO LIKELY CHRISTENING (OR BIRTH) EN-TRY APPEARS IN THE PARISH REGISTERS OR BISHOP'S TRANSCRIPTS OF THE BIRTHPLACE, AND NONE IS FOUND IN THE NONCONFORMIST RECORDS OF THE AREA; SEARCH-ES IN THE PROBATE RECORDS PRODUCED NEGATIVE RESULTS.

A supposed or stated place of birth is not necessarily the place of christening or registration. It is also true that the births of some children were not registered anywhere and were not christened. Statements by ancestors or other as to birthplace are, in many cases, *assumptions* based on the following:

i.   The family moved into the parish shortly *after* the birth of the ancestor who grew up believing he had been born there.

ii. The parents resided in the parish or the stated birthplace before and after the birth, but the ancestor was born during the parents' temporary sojourn elsewhere or while the mother was away on a visit. It is not unusual to be born at the home of grandparents in another parish and later record that parish as a birthplace, but the christening and subsequent registration taking place after the mother's return to her home parish. This is difficult to prove, especially when research has not advanced sufficiently to identify the mother's maiden surname and the names and whereabouts of her parents.

iii. The child was born in the stated place of birth, but taken to another parish, perhaps the residence of grandparents, for the christening and consequent recording.
For example, the parish registers of *Henfield, Sussex,* contains the following christening record:

12 Apr 1811 Mary Ann daughter of James and Naomi Hodges recd. born 24 Aug 1810 *priv. bap at Ashurst* same month. recd at

same place Dec 6. (Ashurst is a neighboring parish. Mary Ann was christened at Henfield the same day as her brother who was born 1 March 1811)

iv. The closest well-known town or city may be listed as a birthplace. Thus a person stated to be born in Norwich was actually born and christened in a small parish outside of the city.

v. The census enumerator or other recorder was misinformed or misheard, and consequently miswrote what he thought was said as to the place of birth.

vi. In cases of illegitimacy or the premature death of the father, a child could be registered under some other surname. See item xi of Procedure #1.

The short search in the registers of the stated birthplace from five years before the stated birth year until the year of marriage of the ancestor may disclose christening and burials of persons bearing the same surname. The information should be prepared into family groups and an analysis of the findings might disclose:

i. Family groups in which there is a sufficient gap in the recordings of the children to include the possible missing record of birth of the ancestor. If, however, the birth and christening record of the ancestor is not registered anywhere, proof of such a connection would be impossible to obtain from christening or birth records alone.

ii. Family groups in which the information on parents and children is far from complete, indicating that additional events of birth, marriage, and death probably took place elsewhere.

When similar searches are made in the registers of adjoining or surrounding parishes and those connected with the known occupations of the ancestors, this information should be listed and prepared into family groups for analysis that might disclose:

A comparison between the family groups prepared from registers of nearby or associated parishes which might show christenings, marriages, and burials, where the parents are of the same names, and the dates of the events fit, without conflict, into what appears to be the record of one family. It is then necessary to show that the circumstantial evidence demonstrates that it is possible for the parents in one parish to have moved to another and are the same persons residing in the other parish.

All the procedures listed in Procedure #1 should also be followed.

PROCEDURE NUMBER FOUR

Finding the birth or christening records for the husband and wife. Record of their marriage is known, but does not provide information as to a place of birth.

In a marriage entry a *place of residence* is sometimes given. This should be borne in mind as searches are made. In some instances the place of residence proves to be the place of birth (more true for women than men) but in other instances it is a residence of a few weeks or so.

Any age at a dated event should be used to calculate the probable birth years of the couple. If the marriage was not stated to be "after banns," consider checking for a possible marriage bond and allegation that might contain details of ages and consent of parents. Even though the marriage entry did not state that either party was widowed, consider this a possibility. Most marriage entries before the passing of the Marriage Act of 1753 do not record the marital status of the bride and groom, and even after 1754, when this specific information was called for, many records fail to include these vital details. It is thus possible for the groom to be a widower and possibly older than expected, and for the bride to be married in her *widowed surname*, making the following essential:

> Study all entries of the bride's surname and watch for a family group where the birth of the last of the recorded children is within a year or two prior to her marriage.[40] If the record of the burial of the father of these children is also previous to her marriage date, this is helpful circumstantial evidence.

To find the births or christenings of the bridegroom and bride, searches will first be made in the registers and other records of the parish where the marriage took place, and where the children of the marriage were born and christened, as well as any place of residence given at marriage.

    i. For the husband, allow that he could have been aged 15 years at the date of marriage, and aged 70 years at the birth of his last known child.

    ii. For the wife, allow that she could have been aged 15 years at the date of marriage, and aged 50 years at the birth of her last known child.

        For example, John Smith and Mary Brown married 13 May 1754. Their last known child was christened or born in 1764.

The period to search for the birth or christening of the husband John Smith will be: 1754-15 = 1739

1764-70 = 1694 Therefore search 1694-1739

---

[40]*Ibid.,* see vol. 1, p. 222 for Ann Thrussell, vol. 1, p. 183 for Isabella Varcoe formerly Pearse, and vol. 2, p. 142 for Eleanor Woodhouse.

The period to search for the birth or christening of the wife **Mary** Brown will be: 1754-15 = 1739

1764-50 = 1714 Therefore search 1714-1739

All parishes within a five mile radius (and those associated with a known and similar occupation) should be searched to find any christening or birth entries of children who might qualify as candidates to consider as ancestral. If the searches provide more than one probable entry for an ancestor, and probate or other records do not clarify the situation, it is necessary to trace the ancestry of each one to determine whether they have common ancestry (as in Procedure #2).

If the above parishes do not produce a possible record, the search will be extended to include:

i. Consideration of the frequency of the surname as disclosed through indexes, such as Boyd's marriage indexes, probate court calendar indexes, etc.

ii. A study of the map and outlining of further searches in wider areas or based upon occupational considerations.

Occupations are important identifiers and often provide the supporting evidence required. They must be considered as a help to find or eliminate a probable ancestral christening or birth record. The finding of a potter or a merchant dealing in earthenware in an area some considerable distance from the national center where such goods are manufactured might be a clue leading to the discovery of the center of the industry and the consequent searching of the records of an entirely different locality from that in which the ancestor resided.[41]

Sailors from merchant and navy ships are known to have had children born in one seaport and christened in another. The same holds true of a soldier whose children were born while his regiment was stationed in one town, or while he was "on the march," and christened in another place where the soldier was stationed or through which he passed. In many instances the wives and children of soldiers and sailors followed these servicemen from one station to another.

It is clear that a rule regarding searching adjoining parishes must be extended to consider the records of churches in areas of interest according to the occupation of the ancestral family, of seaports for sailors and fishermen, and any place that might be important to military establishments and the wanderings of soldiers and their families. The

---

[41]The 1841 census of St. Stephen, Devon, shows Ed Eardley, by occupation a chinaman (i.e., an earthenware dealer), not born in Devonshire. In 1838 at Exeter was married Thomas son of Thomas Eardley, a china dealer. Their ancestry was not from the south-west of England. Their occupations suggested the Potteries in North Staffordshire where earthenware manufacturing is centered, and their pedigree was picked up in Staffordshire.

same holds true in mountainous and moorland areas where the parishes along the same valleys and highways should be searched in addition to adjoining parishes.

When any probable entry is found, it is still essential to search parishes within a five mile area to discover whether or not the child christened was buried unmarried, or married some other person. Bear in mind the eliminating process in Procedures 1, 2, 3. When any conflicting entry is found and cannot be eliminated as possibilities, it is impossible to accept any particular entry as ancestral.

PROCEDURE NUMBER FIVE

Searching for the Marriage Record of the parents of known children, the marriage having taken place before 1 *July* 1837.

If a child in the family was born after July 1837, a search must be made for the birth record for that child in order to secure or confirm the maiden surname of the mother. When all children were born before 1837 it is usual to find only the first given name of the mother recorded in the christening (or birth) records of children listed in church records. There are many registers prior to 1813 that do not list any name at all for the mother; on the other hand there are a few parish registers that record considerable information, but this is rare.

If the registers of the parishes in which the family had residential connections do not disclose the ancestral marriage, and banns publications either do not record an intention to marry or are not extant, then the following procedures and notes should be studied:

    i. Generally speaking the marriage laws of England and Wales permitted the marriage to take place anywhere convenient to those concerned, provided that the legal requirements were filled.[42] Sometimes this meant a minimum of four weeks residence in a parish. In other cases the purchase of a marriage license from the local or higher jurisdictions permitted the wedding to take place almost anywhere appropriate for the occasion.[43]

   ii. The occupation of the husband and the geography and topography of the locality must be considered.[44]

  iii. Marriage indexes such as those of Percival Boyd could be consulted. Bearing these points in mind, each parish in the area will need to be considered.

---

[42]See vol. 1, pp. 206-212.
[43]*Ibid.,* pp. 211-212, 223-224.
[44]Occupation should also include social status. The "gentry" married at fashionable places, similar to the marriage of Thomas Mountford in 1679 at St. Martin in the Fields, Westminster, London. See vol. 1, pp. 224-226.

It was not permissible for nonconformists to marry except at the parish church, particularly between 1754 and 1837, so marriages of such couples will usually be found in the registers of a parish church near where they resided. In Quaker registers, however, many marriages are recorded. It is possible that persons married as Quakers had children recorded in registers of another denomination, especially if either the bride or the groom was not a Quaker. It would be wise, therefore, to search Quaker marriage registers when the marriage cannot be found in the Church of England registers.

The waterman plying a barge along the hundreds of miles of canals perhaps met his bride somewhere along the route. The soldier could have married near to the camp where he was temporarily stationed, and this could easily be in Ireland or in some overseas territory. A sailor could have married in any port in which his ship had anchored. Residents of mountainous country or along wide rivers without bridges usually married in their own valley or side of the river. The market town was often the place where young people from villages miles distant would first meet as they brought their farm produce to be marketed.

A study of the history of the locality might disclose that a nearby large town was an attraction as a place to marry, as was Middleton, Lancashire.[45] There were also fashionable churches, such as St. George, Hanover Square, and St. Martin in the Fields, both situated in the City of Westminster, London.

The issue of a marriage license resulted in the creation of documentation in the registry of the jurisdiction concerned. These records are usually centralized in the diocesan office but may have been transferred to the county record office, and some have already been made available on microfilm. A listing of those printed, complete up to 1960, is given in *Genealogical Research in England and Wales*, Volume 2, Chapter 9. For example, if a marriage took place before 1770 in Nottinghamshire, and a reference was not found in Boyd's *Miscellaneous Marriage Index*, then a search should be made in the index for the marriage bonds and allegations for the Archdeaconry of Nottingham and several Peculiar Courts, printed for 1577 to 1770.

The period of time over which a search for a marriage should be made is:

a. When a calculated year of birth is known, assume that the marriage took place between the time when the youngest spouse became fifteen years of age and one year *after* the birth or christening of the first known child. Bear in mind a possible five-year discrepancy in the calculated year of birth.

---

[45]See vol. 1, p. 208.

For example, suppose John and Mary Smith had only one known child christened in 1754 and it was known that Mrs. Mary Smith was born (by calculation from an age at an event) about 1730. The period to search for the marriage would be:

$$1754 + 1 = 1755$$
$$1725 + 15 = 1740 \text{ Therefore search } 1740\text{-}1755$$

Always use the *earliest* calculated year of birth if more than one is determined from information gathered.

b. When there is no calculated year of birth, assume that the couple were at least sixteen years of age at the time of the birth of their first known child. For the mother, assume that she was at least fifty years of age at the birth of the last child, and that the father was at least seventy years of age. Take both years as the period extremes and search back to the earliest date on the assumption that the marriage more than likely took place about the time of the birth of the first child.

For example the first known child was born or christened 1754, the last known child was born or christened 1770.
The period to search would be:

For the WIFE $1754 + 1 = 1755$
$1770 - 34 \ (50 - 16) = 1736$ Therefore search 1755 back to 1736 working backwards.

For the HUSBAND $1754 + 1 = 1755$
$1770 - 54 \ (70 - 16) = 1716$ Therefore search 1755 back to 1716 working backwards.

As a further example suppose the first known child was born or christened in 1754 and was the only known child and therefore becomes the last known child.

For the WIFE $1754 + 1 = 1755$
$1754 - 34 = 1720$ Therefore search 1755 back to 1720 working backwards.

For the HUSBAND $1754 + 1 = 1755$
$1754 - 54 = 1700$ Therefore search 1755 back to 1700 working backwards.

Note that the less the number of known children the wider the period in which the marriage could have taken place. If both birth and christening dates are known, always use the birth dates as a basis for determining the period in which to search.

PROCEDURE NUMBER SIX

Searching for the Death or Burial of an adult, before 1 *July* 1837.

Ages at death are beneficial in calculating a probable birth year. Since January 1813 all parish registers call for the alleged age at death, and a few before that time recorded this valuable information. It is stressed that burial registers must be searched in an effort to identify the record of death and burial for adults so that this age at death may be learned.

Not only the burial registers but the inscriptions on monuments inside the church and on tombstones in churchyards and cemeteries should be searched. The presence of additional burial grounds opened in the generation of the ancestral family being compiled, together with nonconformist burial grounds, must be investigated.[46]

PROCEDURE NUMBER SEVEN

Searching for the Death or Burial of an infant.

Every effort must be made to determine whether children died young, and particularly if they died unmarried, or if they died before reaching their eighth birthday.[47]

It is usually quite difficult to identify burials of persons prior to 1837, a lot depending upon how much information the church record contains. Whenever possible, burial entries should be matched with christenings and births, but in most parishes there will remain entries that cannot be identified. Some of these may relate to children christened elsewhere or who died unbaptized. Many nonconformists registered their children's births with their own denominational minister, but had funerals conducted in the churchyard of the parish Church of England, or the local cemetery. Consequently, corresponding birth entries are not always to be found in the registers of the place of burial. This is another good reason for searching wide periods in the registers of several parishes.

If the child died after July 1837, the records of deaths registered with the Civil Registration should be searched to find the death of such a child and particularly to discover whether the death took place before its eighth birthday.[47]

---

[46]See vol. 1, p. 38-39, 122, 142, 143, 193.
[47]See *Genealogical Instruction Manual* (Salt Lake City: Genealogical Society, 1964), Section 3, page 36, regarding compiling of L.D.S. family group records only.

PROCEDURE NUMBER EIGHT

Pedigree Research in Cities and Towns having more than one Parish.

In many towns and cities there is more than one ancient parish church.[48] No pedigree should be considered correct and the family group records complete until the parish registers or Bishop's Transcripts of *ALL* the parishes in that city or town have been searched, as well as the registers of all the nonconformist (including Quakers) congregations, and Roman Catholics where available. The periods involved will be the same as those already listed. The five mile rule of searching also applies.

PROCEDURE NUMBER NINE

Ancestral Research in London.

When "born or lived in London" is found in a pedigree, it is difficult, if the dates involved are prior to July 1837, to have immediate success in finding records of the family in the Metropolis.[49] The City of London is less than one square mile in area, but there were more than 100 parish churches within it.[50] To this must be added many parishes just outside the city making a total of about 180.

Since 1889 the modern County of London, covering 117 square miles, was organized by grouping together the twenty-nine towns and cities encircling and including that ancient city. The following list shows the number of ancient parishes within these two cities and twenty-seven boroughs (towns) together with (in parentheses) the name of the former county in which each was geographically situated before 1889:

City of London, 112 parishes, and a number of precincts, liberties and Inns of Court.

City of Westminster (Middlesex), 13 parishes.

Boroughs of:	*No. of Parishes*
Battersea (Surrey)	1
Bermondsey (Surrey)	5
Bethnal Green (Middlesex)	1
Camberwell (Surrey)	1
Chelsea (Middlesex)	1

---

[48]See Vol. 2, page 197 under "Ancient Parishes," and Chap. 9, where under the name of each county is listed the names of those towns where there was more than one parish church prior to 1813 but this listing does not include parishes with chapels of ease.

[49]For information on London see Vol. 2, pp. 264-269, 253-256, 289-291, 238-241.

[50]See Vol. 2, pp. 366-368, for a map of part of the old City of London and an almost complete list of ancient parish churches within the old city itself, but *not* including Westminster and the twenty-seven boroughs.

Deptford (Kent)	2
Finsbury (Middlesex)	3
Fulham (Middlesex)	3
Greenwich (Kent)	3
Hackney (Middlesex)	1
Hammersmith (Middlesex)	1
Hampstead (Middlesex)	1
Holborn (Middlesex)	4
Islington (Middlesex)	1
Kensington (Middlesex)	1
Lambeth (Surrey)	1
Lewisham (Kent)	2
Paddington (Middlesex)	1
Poplar (Middlesex)	3
St. Marylebone (Middlesex)	1
St. Pancras (Middlesex)	1
Shoreditch (Middlesex)	1
Southwark (Surrey)	4
Stepney (Middlesex)	7
Stoke Newingon (Middlesex)	1
Wandsworth (Surrey)	5
Woolwich (Kent)	3

In 1965 considerable changes will be made in the boundaries of the *County of London*. The new area will include not only the above twenty-eight Metropolitan Boroughs, combined into fewer but larger units, but will incorporate within it all the present county of Middlesex, and parts of the present counties of Surrey, Kent and Essex. There will then be 32 boroughs and the City of London within the county.

LIST OF EXISTING AREAS IN LONDON

Name of Place	Former London Borough (if any)	Name of County before March 1965	Name of Borough in Which Situated after March 1965
Acton	——	Middx	Ealing, Lond.
Barking (western part)	——	Essex	Newham, Lond.
Barking (eastern part)	——	Essex	Barking, Lond.
Barnes	——	Surrey	Richmond Upon Thames, Lond.
Barnet	——	Herts	Barnet, Lond.
Battersea	Battersea	London	Wandsworth, Lond.
Beckenham	——	Kent	Bromley, Lond.
Beddington & Wallington	——	Surrey	Sutton, Lond.
Bermondsey	Bermondsey	London	Southwark, Lond.
Bethnal Green	Bethnal Green	London	Tower Hamlets, Lond.
Bexley	——	Kent	Bexley, Lond.

Name of Place	Former London Borough (if any)	Name of County before March 1965	Name of Borough in Which Situated after March 1965
Brentford & Chiswick	——	Middx	Hounslow, Lond.
Bromley	——	London	Bromley, Lond.
Camberwell	Camberwell	London	Southwark, Lond.
Carshalton	——	Surrey	Sutton, Lond.
Cheam (Sutton and)	——	Surrey	Sutton, Lond.
Chelsea	Chelsea	London	Kensington & Chelsea, Lond.
Chigwell (southern part)	——	Essex	Redbridge, Lond.
Chingford	——	Essex	Waltham Forest, Lond.
Chiselhurst & Sidcup (northern part))	——	Kent	Bexley, Lond.
(southern part)		Kent	Bromley, Lond.
Chiswick (Brentford &)	——	Middx	Hounslow, Lond.
Coombe (Malden and)	——	Surrey	Kingston Upon Thames, Lond.
Coulsden and Purley	——	Surrey	Croydon, Lond.
Crayford	——	Kent	Bexley, Lond.
Croydon	——	Surrey	Croydon, Lond.
Dagenham (northern part)	——	Essex	Redbridge, Lond.
Dagenham (southern part)	——	Essex	Barking, Lond.
Deptford	Deptford	London	Lewisham, Lond.
Ealing	——	Middx	Ealing, Lond.
East Barnet	——	Herts	Barnet, Lond.
East Ham	——	Essex	Newham, Lond.
Edmonton	——	Middx	Enfield, Lond.
Enfield	——	Middx	Enfield, Lond.
Erith	——	Kent	Bexley, Lond.
Feltham	——	Middx	Hounslow, Lond.
Finchley	——	Middx	Barnet, Lond.
Finsbury	Finsbury	London	Islington, Lond.
Friern Barnet	——	Middx	Barnet, Lond.
Fulham	Fulham	London	Hammersmith, Lond.
Greenwich	Greenwich	London	Greenwich, Lond.
Hackney	Hackney	London	Hackney, Lond.
Hammersmith	Hammersmith	London	Hammersmith, Lond.
Hampstead	Hampstead	London	Camden, Lond.
Harlington (Hayes &)	——	Middx	Hillingdon, Lond.
Harrow	——	Middx	Harrow, Lond.
Hayes & Harlington	——	Middx	Hillingdon, Lond.
Hendon	——	Middx	Barnet, Lond.
Heston & Isleworth	——	Middx	Hounslow, Lond.
Holborn	Holborn	London	Camden, Lond.
Hornchurch	——	Essex	Havering, Lond.
Hornsey	——	London	Haringey, Lond.
Ilford	——	Essex	Redbridge, Lond.
Isleworth (Heston &)	——	Middx	Hounslow, Lond.
Islington	Islington	London	Islington, Lond.
Kensington	Kensington	London	Kensington & Chelsea, Lond.
Kingston-Upon-Thames	——	Surrey	Kingston Upon Thames, Lond.
Lambeth	Lambeth	London	Lambeth, Lond.
Lewisham	Lewisham	London	Lewisham, Lond.
Leyton	——	Essex	Waltham Forest, Lond.

Name of Place	Former London Borough (if any)	Name of County before March 1965	Name of Borough in Which Situated after March 1965
Malden and Coombe	——	Surrey	Kingston Upon Thames, Lond.
Merton and Morden	——	Surrey	Merton, Lond.
Mitcham	——	Surrey	Merton, Lond.
Morden (Merton &)	——	Surrey	Merton, Lond.
Orpington	——	Kent	Bromley, Lond.
Paddington	Paddington	London	Westminster, Lond.
Penge	——	Kent	Bromley, Lond.
Poplar	Poplar	London	Tower Hamlets, Lond.
Richmond	——	Surrey	Richmond Upon Thames, Lond.
Romford	——	Essex	Havering, Lond.
Ruislip-Northwood	——	Middx	Hillingdon, Lond.
St. Marylebone	St. Marylebone	London	Westminster, Lond.
St. Pancras	St. Pancras	London	Camden, Lond.
Shoreditch	Shoreditch	London	Hackney, Lond.
Sidcup (Chislehurst and)	——		
(northern part)		Kent	Bexley, Lond.
(southern part)		Kent	Bromley, Lond.
Southall	——	Middx	Ealing, Lond.
Southgate	——	Middx	Enfield, Lond.
Southwark	Southwark	London	Southwark, Lond.
Stepney	Stepney	London	Tower Hamlets, Lond.
Stoke Newington	Stoke Newington	London	Hackney, Lond.
Surbiton	——	Surrey	Kingston Upon Thames, Lond.
Sutton and Cheam	——	Surrey	Sutton, Lond.
Tottenham	——	Middx	Haringey, Lond.
Twickenham	——	Middx	Richmond Upon Thames, Lond.
Uxbridge	——	Middx	Hillingdon, Lond.
Wallington (Beddington &)	——	Surrey	Sutton, Lond.
Walthamstow	——	Essex	Waltham Forest, Lond.
Wandsworth	Wandsworth		
(eastern part)		London	Lambeth, Lond.
(western part)		London	Wandsworth, Lond.
Wanstead and Woodford	——	Essex	Redbridge, Lond.
Wembley	——	Middx	Brent, Lond.
West Drayton (Yiewsley &)	——	Middx	Hillingdon, Lond.
West Ham	——	Essex	Newham, Lond.
Westminster	Westminster (City)	London	Westminster, Lond.
Wimbledon	——	Surrey	Merton, Lond.
Willesden	——	Middx	Brent, Lond.
Woodford (Wanstead &)	——	Essex	Redbridge, Lond.
Wood Green	——	Middx	Haringey, Lond.
Woolwich	Woolwich		
(south of Thames)		London	Greenwich, Lond.
(north of Thames)		London	Newham, Lond.
Yiewsley & West Drayton	——	Middx	Hillingdon, Lond.
London (City)	London (City)	London	City of London, Lond.

When the precise parish in which the ancestor might have been born or was resident is unknown, recourse has to be made to directories or other types of indexes that indicate the probable locality associated with the family surname. These include Boyd's marriage indexes, probate court indexes, Freedom of the City and guild company records, indexed obituaries, births and marriages from the *London Times*, Boyd's Citizens of London Indexes, marriage licenses from the various London jurisdictions, and local indexes found in the possession of the many public and private libraries in the metropolis. There is also a privately owned marriage index known as Pallot's Marriage Index, purported to list all marriages from certain London parishes for the period roughly 1789-1837.

If some trace is found of the family within a small locality or street, perhaps such as Fleet Street, City of London, then all the parishes on and adjoining Fleet Street need to be searched first, with consideration being given to the rest of the City. Then the Nonparochial registers of London, a series of records for 193 Nonconformist chapels (including Quakers) within four miles of St. Paul's Cathedral, need to be checked for the locality concerned, as well as the Catholic records where available, Jewish records and the nonconformist records from certain London registries.

When there is no clue as to the parish or town in or near London where the family was born or resided, there is no other alternative but to search the church records of the whole of the cities of London and Westminster and the twenty-seven adjoining boroughs.

PROCEDURE NUMBER TEN

Finding complete families.

When all previously listed requirements or standards have been satisfied and the pedigree extensions depend upon the weight of circumstantial evidence because probate and other records have failed to substantiate the connections, it is still important to search the records of adjoining parishes.

These searches will not only disclose possible conflicts but will often find the records of the birth for children not previously incorporated in the family group records, as well as locating the marriage and death records for other members of the family, sometimes even for the parents.

Before any family groups can be considered, church records should be searched over at least a thirty-five year period, the beginning of this period being the year of marriage of a particular couple. Other couples recorded as bearing children at the beginning and the end of the period searched would have children earlier and later. Their family groups should not be considered complete until appropriate extensions have been made to the search. (See *Genealogical Instruction Manual*, Section 9, page, 6.)

Suggestions to Instructor

Several lessons are involved in Chapters 9 and 10.

This is different subject material from Chapters 1-8 but is most important. Be sure that the class members understand each standard and procedure clearly. Then lead them to realize that all the existing sources which could have provided positive proof were searched but failed to provide proof thus calling for the special procedures described.

Feel free to use added examples of problems on the blackboard so that class members have a clear picture of the areas that must be searched and the types of records that must be eliminated, before a circumstantial conclusion can be reached.

INDEX